Two's Company but Three's a Crowd?

Assistants in Music Therapy Sessions

Britta Schmidt-Robyn

Two's Company but Three's a Crowd?

Assistants in Music Therapy Sessions

Bibliographische Information der Deutschen Nationalbibliothek
Die Deutsche Nationalbibliothek verzeichnet diese Publikation in der Deutschen Nationalbibliographie; detaillierte bibliographische Daten sind im Internet über http//:dnb.d-nb.de abrufbar.

Copyright © 2008 Britta Schmidt
Herstellung und Verlag: Books on Demand GmbH, Norderstedt
Layout und Titelfoto: Julie Robyn

Alle Rechte vorbehalten. Dieses Buch darf – auch auszugsweise – nicht ohne die schriftliche Zustimmung der Autorin kopiert werden.
Die Inhalte dieser Publikation wurden sorgfältig recherchiert, aber dennoch haftet die Autorin nicht für Folgen von Irrtümern, mit denen der vorliegende Text behaftet sein könnte.

ISBN 9783837017335

Published in Germany 2008 by Books on Demand GmbH, Norderstedt.
All rights reserved.
Copyright © 2008 Britta Schmidt
Layout and title photo: Julie Robyn

With thanks to all the people who contributed to this book.

Contents

Introduction — 9

1. The assistant's role — 15

2. Relationship matters — 29

Influence of the assistant on the client's behaviour and emotions — 30

Influence of the assistant on the therapist's views of the client and emotions towards the client — 36

Transference and countertransference — 39

The wish to prove oneself — 49

Envy — 61

3. Issues around the work setup — 65

Boundaries and confidentiality — 65

Clash of contexts — 70

4. Issues around the therapy process — 77

The luxury of not knowing — 77

The fine balance between hope, expectations and unconditional acceptance — 79

Whose norms? Whose limits? — 85

5. Working through, working with or working to minimise? 93

German summary/Deutsche Zusammenfassung 101

References 115

Appendix I: Questionnaire for music therapists 117

Appendix II: Questionnaire for music therapy assistants 121

Appendix III: Leaflet about music therapy for assistants 123

Introduction

Peter has exhausted himself. He has played two big drums piled on top of each other for twenty-five minutes, banging them as hard as he could, and shouting as loud as he could. Peter, who is seventeen and has Downs' syndrome, had been referred to me by his school for severe challenging behaviour that led him to attack staff and other children and to destroy furniture. Although I have not felt safe enough to see Peter on his own without the protection of another staff member in the same room, music therapy with him has felt particularly effective, appropriate and satisfying. It has helped him experience that energy and emotion are not 'bad' but that they need channelling, and that there are different ways of letting them out. Work with Peter has been very inspirational and inspiring, very emotional, explosive but containable, with incredibly rich moments of vividness and moments of calm.

The assistant, who plays a motherly role not only for Peter, but also for a lot of other children and staff in the school, comes in with him, sits in a corner and gives me warm, encouraging smiles.

Now Peter is exhausted. He has let off all his steam, and with a tired and happy glance over to me by the piano, he lets himself sink down onto the floor, lying on his back, still maintaining eye contact.

What follows is a meaningful silence that seems to contain understanding that we can be noisy together, but that we can also hold silence together. It feels like a key moment in our work together.

Suddenly the assistant rises from her chair, searching for her bag. "Just while he isn't doing anything", she says with a cheerful smile, "I have got these photos of my new grandson... do you want to look at them now?"

A lot has been written about the relationships between therapists and clients, about the role of music within these relationships, and about transference and countertransference between therapist and client etc. But what if the relationship involves a third person who is actually present in the room? A person who is part of the therapy but, at the same time, is neither a client, nor a therapist, nor sometimes even in a close relationship with the client? A person whose presence entails separate issues and separate dynamics? What if the therapeutic relationship is not actually a two-way relationship between music therapist and client?

Although many music therapists, especially those working in the area of Special Needs, do a lot of work with assistants present in the same room, it is strange that this area has found little close examination or recognition in music therapy literature or in literature concerning related therapy approaches. This is all the more striking since a third person will, as soon as they are present in the room, have an influence on the relationship and on the dynamics. They will form an integral part of the therapeutic process, even though they may not consciously choose this.

This short book, which is based on my MA dissertation in music therapy that I completed in 2004 at Anglia Polytechnic University in Cambridge, England, includes information gathered from informal and formal interviews with colleagues and talks with music therapy assistants, as well as reflections and case material arising from my own music therapy work.

While working as a music therapist for Bristol Music Space from 2001 to 2004 I regularly visited three Special Needs schools and one Opportunity Group. I often had to work with assistants in my sessions. They were present for a variety of different reasons to do with medical issues, behaviour management support and support with practical issues.

After completing my dissertation, I left England and moved to Berlin, Germany, where I have since been working in various areas, including adult mental health, dementia care and neurology. This has also involved working with assistants such as music therapy trainees, speech therapy trainees or assistant care workers, albeit to a lesser extent.

In order to gain enough relevant information for my 2004 dissertation, I developed a questionnaire that I sent out to about fifty colleagues at the end of 2003. Twenty-three of these questionnaires were filled in and returned to me. The questionnaire included eight questions. These questions concerned their experiences of working with assistants in their sessions, and their approaches to the different aspects of this collaboration

Only two colleagues said that they never worked with assistants in their sessions. However, twenty-one people said that they worked with assistants either all the time, often or sometimes, and they shared their experiences with me. Above all, this indicates one important thing to me: it is not at all uncommon for music therapists to work with a stranger in the room. On the contrary, the overwhelming majority of those people I spoke to said that this way of working was fairly normal for them! In light of this, it seems all the more strange that this subject has found so little recognition in training courses and music therapy literature.

The music therapists who completed the questionnaire worked in a variety of different areas, mostly in Special Needs, but also in mental health, in bereavement care, in palliative care, in homes for elderly people, and in prisons. They worked with a whole range of different age groups, and they had different UK, Dutch and German training backgrounds. At the time of answering the questions, they lived and worked in various areas of England, Scotland, Wales and Germany. They also worked according to a variety of different approaches including person-centred, developmental, psychodynamic, psychoanalytically informed, and behavioural approaches.

In addition to the information gleaned from the questionnaire, I was also fortunate enough to participate in some personal, more in-depth talks with several colleagues. This gave me even more insight into some of the issues that can arise as a result of the presence of an assistant, and helped me to understand the ways in which colleagues have addressed these issues or tried to deal with them.

During 2003 I also talked to several assistants who I had been working with, and asked them about their thoughts, perceptions and ideas. I developed a questionnaire for assistants, which a few of them filled in and handed back to me. More assistants, however, seemed to find it easier to talk to me in person and share their thoughts directly, preferring to help me this way, rather than writing their thoughts down anonymously. I asked all of the assistants what they felt had been their best and their worst experience as a music therapy assistant, and what they thought the music therapist could do in order to improve the work relationship.

In order to avoid the subject being too broad, I have kept to those cases where the extra person was neither another therapist, nor a family member, nor another client.

In order to ensure confidentiality, all names have naturally been changed.

1. The assistant's role

While talking to colleagues and when analysing the responses on the questionnaires, two things became clear to me. Firstly, it struck me just how many different aspects there are to 'assistants in a music therapy session'. There are so many different roles, contexts and reasons for having an assistant in a music therapy session. They could be there to supervise medical issues, to translate between the therapist and the client, or help with behaviour management. They could be there in order to act as a bridge between the therapist and the institution, with the additional task of reporting back to the institution, or they could be there for reasons of their own – they could be a music therapy trainee, for example.

Secondly, it became obvious that as soon as a third person is present, their role within the therapy session needs to be negotiated and this role, in turn, impacts on the therapy process as well as on the therapist's role.

It seems clear that the assistant's presence will almost always challenge our conventional ideas about music therapy and the therapist's role.

About one third of the music therapists stated on the questionnaire that they regarded the assistant to be part of the therapeutic process; about one third said that they felt they were merely an observer of the process. The rest said that this varied according to the situation.

Nine music therapists said that they would, if they could, seek to make the assistant's role as passive and restrained as possible, while four said that they would try and give them an active role. One colleague added the comment that she felt that the assistant's influence was better under control if they had an active rather than a passive role.

Thirteen people said that they would sometimes give the assistant a musical role, i.e. let them play an instrument or sing, while five ruled this out. Ten music therapists said that they had sometimes allowed an assistant to contribute, however, only four stated that they would ever *encourage* an assistant to contribute.

Only three therapists said that they would work through issues that had arisen through the presence of the assistant during the session. Fourteen said that they tended to do this after the session, or not at all.

Most therapists said that they would acknowledge the assistant's presence; thirteen said that they would do this musically; sixteen said that they would do this verbally. Two music therapists said that they would never acknowledge the assistant's presence in the session, verbally or musically.

Most colleagues also made it clear that these answers are just tendencies, and that these will vary according to the particular situation and person. Most people answered with 'sometimes', 'often' or 'rarely', rather than with 'always' or 'never'.

As one can see from these answers, there seems to be a huge variety in the approach music therapists take towards assistants, and the roles which they are given, and this, in turn, will impact differently on the influence that the assistant's presence has on the therapeutic process.

So is there any way in which these many roles can be categorised and pigeonholed?

In order to have some basic categories to work with, I have defined three different options. However, later I will show that in practice, these roles will rarely ever be as simple and straightforward.

Firstly, the assistant could have the role of another carer or even co-therapist. This could apply if they are a teacher, a music therapy student, or an assistant nurse. Secondly, the person could have the role of another client, which could be the case if the work addresses the relationship between the client and the role or institution the assistant represents, or, on a more personal level, between the client and the assistant themselves. In many cases, this could be ambivalent as the assistant could have both roles at the same time.

Thirdly, the extra person might be neither another carer nor another client, but their role might be independent from those two. This might happen, for example, if he or she has come to watch the session in order to learn about music therapy, but is not directly concerned with the client or the process itself.

In the third case, the assistant's role could be one of two things. The assistant could either take a role which is actively involved in the music therapy work and process. This might mean that the assistant is clearly part of the therapeutic process and relationship. Secondly, the therapist could seek to make the assistant's role as held back and passive as possible. In many cases, the assistant's role will work out somewhere in the middle, or will be in constant need of negotiation. Often, issues around the assistant's presence may stem from a need to negotiate this question, and the implications that follow from this. Again, I will be dealing with issues relating to this, in more depth in the chapters to follow.

In most cases, however, these roles will be blurred. People may take more than one of those roles, or their role will change or will emerge only as the music therapy work progresses. Sometimes, if the necessity arises to clarify and think about the particular role the person has, as well as what this means to the music therapy work and whether the person's role is helpful or not, this might be the start of some deeper thinking about the process and about what is happening in the room. Clarifying a person's role might in itself become a door that leads to more in-depth reflection on the music therapy work.

However, it seems important to bear in mind that, even in cases where the set up of the assistant's role had been very clear and straightforward, the reality of the session may show that this turns into something totally different.

One of the clients I saw was a girl with profound multiple learning disabilities. Emma needed a specifically trained carer with her at all times, day and night. The role of this carer had clearly been set up to be a medical supervisor. The assistant was not meant to take any active role within the therapeutic relationship, but she was intended to just sit and watch and step in only if there was a problem with Emma's breathing. At the beginning of the work, I had a chat with the assistant, briefly told her about music therapy, what it was going to be for and that there wasn't really much she would need to do except for sitting back and relaxing for half an hour, while I was working with Emma. The assistant would pull her chair a little bit away from Emma and just make sure she had Emma's oxygen supply and breathing tube well in sight.

However, Emma, as she was used to having the assistant there with her every minute of the day, did not start focusing on the music therapy, as I had hoped. Since Emma was not able to breathe through her nose, she had to wear a breathing tube that went through the front of her neck, which had an air filter attached to it. In due course, she started grabbing the lid and pulling it out, so that the assistant had to keep putting it back on. This game increased in intensity and soon turned out to be way more interesting to Emma than music therapy. The assistant had hardly put the lid back, when Emma would grab it again, pull it out and throw it onto the floor.

I tried having the assistant sit back right next to her, which did, however, not solve the problem as Emma was still a lot more focused on the assistant than the music therapy work I was trying to offer to her.

I addressed this by changing my session from a relatively slow speed and allowing Emma a lot of space to take the lead, into a much faster pace and a lot more stimulation. Eventually, this approach worked and Emma started taking an interest in the songs I offered, in the piano and in the guitar that was held out for her to strum.

However, the therapeutic work had had to take a completely different route from how it had originally been intended, because of the assistant's role not working out as it had been planned.

A colleague told me about another situation in which she worked with a male, adult client who had extremely challenging behaviour, and who could potentially be very dangerous if attacking anybody working with him. My colleague therefore worked with a care assistant in the session. Since her client had a tendency to increase challenging behaviour if he felt that he was performing for an audience, she asked the assistant to pretend she wasn't watching and to look out of the window some of the time, or possibly bring a book to read. However, this had the opposite effect on the client. He tried to force the assistant's attention by playing louder and louder music, until he finally broke an ocean drum just by playing it hard with his fists. In due course, my colleague changed the assistant's role and actively involved her into the process and the music making, which turned out to be helpful to the situation, and no serious incidents of challenging behaviour occurred as the work went on

While collecting case material, starting to think about assistant – therapist situations in more depth and increasingly talking to colleagues about their experiences, I was struck by the fact that, in a lot of cases, issues stemmed from a clash between how the assistant's role had been *intended or set up*, and how their role *turned out to be in reality*. I also found this supported by communication with assistants.

When asking assistants about what they found difficult about being a music therapy assistant, and about what the music therapist could have done to make their job easier or more enjoyable, it turned out that wherever issues occurred, they often stemmed from the need to clearly define the assistant's role, from the assistant feeling unsure what they were supposed to do, or from situations in which their role, as it had been defined, did not work out for the music therapy work.

One major issue seems to be the fact that the original definition of an assistant's role can clash with the way it turns out in reality, once the work has started.

For example, an assistant could be present for a purely practical reason, but then turn out to have a major influence on the therapeutic relationship. An assistant could be in the room to help the client's behaviour management, but their pure presence could foster the client's challenging behaviour and provoke them into their tried and tested ways of behaving, because the assistant might trigger the same buttons which they were used to being triggered.

It may be that a person's role is meant to be that of observer, but their presence may actually turn out to have a huge influence on the session. The child might keep running up to them, making contact or offering them instruments; or the client might suddenly behave very differently. In this case, a decision will need to be made as to how therapist and assistant should address this. Will the assistant respond to the client? Will they pretend they have not noticed?

If they do respond, their response will be an integral part of what has happened in the session this time. It will inevitably become part of the therapeutic path. If they choose not to respond, then this will have consequences too. The client might feel very rejected by this, a situation which is quite contrary to what music therapy is likely to have been set up for. The client might not actively try and make contact, but the extra person's presence may still have some influence on their emotions or on the therapist's behaviour.

An assistant's role will often turn out to differ from how it had been originally intended or set up. The question that arises for the therapist, then, is how to deal with this. Is the change welcome? Is it an improvement to the original idea? Does it throw up problems or unwelcome issues? Would it be a good idea to address those, and if so, in which way?

Another issue can be a clash between the therapist's definition of the assistant's role, and the assistant's understanding of their own role. This could simply be due to a lack of communication, and could in some cases be easily rectified. Most of the colleagues I spoke to have had situations where assistants, though with the best of intentions, thought their task was to support the therapist in making the client play the instruments as much as possible, and 'helped' by making comments like "Go on – play that drum, be a good boy", or by even taking the client's hand and making them play an instrument.

In many cases, clear communication can resolve most of the potential problems around unclear or confusing roles and the particular sharing of responsibilities in the session.

It is also important to bear in mind that it may be the very need to clarify a person's role, or to analyse the blurring of different roles which the assistant has started taking, that leads the therapist to insights about the work and about the therapeutic process.

In one of my groups which I ran in a Special Needs School, I worked with an assistant who, having finished her music degree, had only just left university, and had started working as a learning support assistant. She had put an interest in a future career as a Special Needs teacher on her application form, and it seemed to make a lot of sense for the school to allocate her the role of assistant for my group.

I had asked for an assistant because the group of four teenage children was very lively and involved two boys who had a history and reputation of being particularly difficult. In the previous school term, I had run this group with an assistant who had primarily focused on behaviour management, while my role was to deal with emotions, and to provide structure, musical support and empathy.

The new assistant, Lisa, turned out to be very quiet and shy – more so than any of the children in her charge. She would move her chair slightly out of the circle, as if unconsciously to tell me that she did not want to be part of the group but would rather be just a silent audience, as unnoticeable as possible. She would not contribute verbally or musically. It soon turned out that the former division of roles with the assistant as the behaviour manager and me as the emphatic therapist would no longer work. During the first few sessions, Lisa did not really take up any role at all, except that of quiet observer.

After a few weeks, I had managed to establish a few minimal boundaries. The group had now understood that they could not hit others, throw instruments around the room, get up and pull boxes out of shelves, or pull each other's hair. With a lot of effort, I redirected the high amounts of energy and emotion into musical improvisations. Only gradually did the group get to a stage where screaming and hitting had turned into incredibly lively music.

However, although initially there had been a lot more behaviour problems than in the presence of the previous assistant, our music had now also changed. It seemed to have a different quality to it, a different kind of emotionality and authenticity. When I introduced a session structure which allowed the students in turn to choose a mood as well as a set of instruments for their piece, I started to feel that the students were now less inhibited and started to be more able to express their emotions directly.

The change of role of the assistant had already made a major difference to the group. However, I still felt that Lisa's role was not satisfying. I felt that her skills and abilities could be used better than this.

I suggested meeting up with her for half an hour before my first client, and to take some time to play music together. Lisa was very pleased, and in the following few weeks, we had several short improvisation sessions during which I encouraged her to make use of her musical and vocal skills, and then to integrate those into the group too.

Over the next few months, Lisa's role changed dramatically. She did, to my surprise, turn out to be an excellent musician and sensitive and skilled improviser. A little bit of boosting her confidence had made a great difference. Lisa also started contributing verbally, by commenting on things which she had observed were going on in the group. She generally did this in a sensitive and intuitive manner.

Lisa's role had changed from being an observer with no own role or agenda towards being a co-therapist. Although she did not take up any responsibilities which were separate from my role, she now supported me in my own role. Lisa and I felt very comfortable with each other, and we both liked the roles we had taken up towards each other.

One day, when one of the boys had a tantrum and I offered him a drum and suggested that we put his anger into a piece of music, I heard, to my surprise, Lisa shout:

"Liam! Behave now! And be happy...!"

I had never heard Lisa shout at any of the students, and her attempt to tell a boy how he ought to feel astonished me hugely, given her previous sensitive and understanding approach to her task.

After the session, I asked Lisa about this comment. Lisa apologised, saying that it had just 'slipped out', then went on to tell me that this was the new behaviour strategy the teacher was using with this boy – to ask him to comply and to display happy, not angry emotions.

My first response was one of disbelief and shock. I went on to explain to Lisa that music therapy was not about telling anybody how to feel, but rather about helping people adequately express any of their feelings, and about helping people own and channel their feelings. I also told Lisa that I myself felt very strongly about client's rights to the full range of their own emotions. Lisa looked thoughtful and nodded in agreement. Then, she told me about her own feelings, and how difficult she found it herself if she was in surroundings where she could not express grief or anger; how much she had herself experienced that feelings can gain power and take over, if they were not given permission or an outlet.

In Lisa's case, the assistant role changed several times during the course of the work. Lisa started off as a passive observer to the process of the group. However, this on its own did have an impact on the group, because it fostered changes. Then, Lisa gradually grew into the role of a co- therapist, through musical and verbal support of what I was doing. During one moment, though, Lisa's role became that of a teacher who told the student what to do. When this was clearly discouraged on my part, Lisa's role changed again – though not within the group but in the music session between her and me – and Lisa almost took the role of another client, referring the situation to her own emotions, telling me about herself and seeking my support.

2. Relationship matters

We all know that in the vast majority of therapeutic approaches, the client – therapist relationship is at the core of the therapy. And, of course, as a consequence, this means that the presence of another person in the session will raise a whole range of issues and questions regarding this client – therapist relationship.

Out of the twenty music therapists who stated on the questionnaire that they had experience of working with assistants in their sessions, nineteen said that they felt the client – therapist relationship was being influenced or changed by another person's presence. Only one person stated that they did not feel the therapeutic relationship was being influenced. Ten therapists said that there was 'always' or 'usually' an influence, eight said this happened 'often' and only one said it was the case 'sometimes'.

Given the fact that the therapeutic relationship is often at the root of the music therapy work, and given that the questionnaire suggests that an assistant's presence does have an impact on the relationship, it seems rather strange that this issue has not so far found any recognition in music therapy literature. In the following, I am going to take a look at a number of ways in which the therapeutic relationship will be affected by the presence of an assistant.

Influence of the assistant on the client's emotions and behaviour

Therapy is supposed to be a neutral space, in which the client can safely explore their emotions, their behaviour patterns, their perceptions of the world, and in which they can make a test run of changed behaviour patterns and world views.

However, as soon as there is an assistant in the room, this is bound to have an influence on the nature of this space. If the assistant is a significant person from the client's life (such as a teacher, learning support assistant or carer), this cannot but impact on this idea greatly. As soon as there is another person in the room, who brings their own preconceptions, their own relationship with the client, their own feelings and views, the space is no longer neutral. This will often affect the client's emotions or behaviour.

In one of the Special Schools I worked in, I saw a girl who had been referred to me for severe challenging behaviour. Over time, Sam had built a whole reputation of being difficult. Almost everybody in school had had some experience with Sam's challenging behaviour. Sam would kick or spit, swear or pull people's hair. Two members of staff had had to go to hospital after having been injured by Sam during one of her outbursts of aggression. It seemed clear that it would not be wise to even attempt to see Sam without another adult present in the room.

Most people's view of Sam, as well as her self-image, seemed largely hooked up with her challenging behaviour. Younger girls were being told "Don't do this – you don't want to be like Sam, do you...?!" When I picked Sam up from her classroom, staff who met us on the way to the music room gave me a sympathetic look and a sigh, saying "Oh dear... have fun."

I found out that Sam's mother, although living with her, had completely rejected her, and that it was her father who talked to her, dealt with her and cared for her. Her father seemed to do whatever he could to protect her mother as well as three siblings from Sam's challenging behaviour.

Sam herself was very aware of people around her and of their reactions and responses. She knew everybody's names, would shout and try to attract people's attention if they walked by, and would often talk about people in her life such as teachers, classroom assistants, other pupils, family. She seemed to be crying out for attention, love and recognition. Her self-image seemed to be connected to challenging behaviour.

My first session with Sam largely consisted of a chat between her and the classroom assistant, who talked to her about her behaviour, and discussed the implications of hair pulling with her, telling Sam how sad and upset she would feel should Sam attempt to grab and pull my hair. This went on until Sam smiled, reached out both her hands and grabbed the assistant's hair with one hand and mine with the other, and pulled us both across the room by our hair. This ended the session, and left me with the conclusion that this could not really be the answer to the way forward.

Before the next session, I asked the assistant not actually to come into the session with Sam, but to sit outside the door, and just to come in if she heard the situation get out of control.

I asked Sam to tell me all about her favourite songs and invited her to try instruments, one after another. Sam, instead, went on to tell me about incidents of challenging behaviour including who she had been swearing at, who she had kicked this morning, and which forms of punishment she had been given for this; while not making any attempt to pull my hair or behave in any difficult way towards me at this moment.

Then, Sam started hiding in her T- shirt, pulling it up all across her face, and eventually lifted up a chair to hide herself from me. At this moment, the assistant, who had watched through the keyhole, opened the door and came in.

"Are you about to throw this chair?!...", she said. "Remember what I told you... no hurting other people... it would make us all very sad!"

It is almost needless to say that at this moment the chair was flung all across the room, and the session ended with swearing and attempts to pull the assistant's hair.

In due course, I tried working with Sam while having an assistant sit in the corner, who I had asked to comment only on Sam's *positive* sides.

However, I soon started to feel that even this did not work out. Even though words can be a strong form of communication, nonverbal communication has a great deal of power too. Of course, Sam would still pick up on the assistant's expectations, on her looks, body language and her anxiety. Often, Sam would glance over to the assistant and start displaying challenging behaviour until she had finally received a response. This went as far as her trying to undress, and trying to throw a drum against the window.

It had become clear that it was the staff's very attitude towards this difficult girl, which actually triggered a lot of the challenging behaviour. The staff's expectations of Sam and her behaviour created just what music therapy had been asked to try and decrease.

What's more: the assistant's presence actually *fostered* Sam's challenging behaviour that it had been meant to protect me from. Obviously, I was in a paradoxical situation. I did not feel able to work with Sam on my own, and run the risk of being physically harmed by her aggressive behaviour. On the other hand, the presence of an audience, especially an audience who brought particular negative expectations, seemed to make Sam's challenging behaviour more likely and ultimately prevented me from being able to work with her in any constructive kind of way. This was the case even when these negative expectations were not explicitly put into words, but when words were chosen so that they tried to express a positive attitude.

Further incidents of Sam's challenging behaviour in the classroom finally made the school buy a panic button, which staff working with her could use at any time. This enabled me to find a solution for this situation.

I started seeing Sam on her own, with the emergency button in my pocket, while two members of staff sat next door, ready to come in should I require any help.

I started by actively praising Sam for every five minutes that she had not been misbehaving. If I felt that Sam was about to start challenging behaviour, I finished the session and praised her for having been so 'good'. Fortunately, staff and teachers supported this approach of mine. Where initially, our sessions took sometimes only three to five minutes, they gradually increased in length until we could do a full session, focusing on Sam's interests and qualities, composing songs about things she liked, talking about her hobbies and generally building on a new sense of identity, which had nothing to do with challenging behaviour.

In this case, assistants had been so traumatised by difficult experiences with Sam that it had become impossible for them to approach her without negative expectations, which helped create Sam's unhelpful sense of self, which was closely connected with challenging behaviour. In this case, the only way out of this was to start working with Sam by herself, and to actively help her replace this self image with a different one, which gradually also changed her reputation in school and the way staff responded to her.

Influence of the assistant on the therapist's views of and emotions towards the client

We must not forget that it is not only the client's emotions that will be influenced by the presence of another person in the room. The therapist can just as well find his or her feelings, views and, as a consequence, sometimes even behaviour, influenced by having an audience present.

On the questionnaire, twelve out of twenty music therapists stated that the presence of an assistant did sometimes have an impact on their perception of the client, or that at least they felt this was a risk.

Again, this could happen on a conscious or on an unconscious level. And, as mentioned in the previous chapter, this could be triggered not only by words and by what is being said – subtle things like body language, looks, tone of voice and gestures can be very powerful as well. Those things could have a lot of power especially if they remain on the unconscious level.

If the music therapist is very conscious of his or her degree of vulnerability to being influenced this way, as well as to the ways in which this is most likely to happen, the risk may be reduced. However, the process may be very subtle and difficult to spot.

If the assistant comes into the room looking relaxed and smiling at the client, then the therapist is likely to feel very different about the client than if the assistant brought the same client, looking stressed out and tired and giving the client angry looks.

It would be extremely difficult not to be influenced by this and not to add this observation to the mental image one is forming about the client.

It may sometimes be one of the benefits of therapy that the therapist is separate from the usual context and sheltered off from the rest of the client's life, so that a space is created that is different and free from preconceived ideas about the client. Therapy can then be a space in which the client can try out new roles and safely explore their identity without being influenced by prejudices and expectations on how they should behave or who they should be, or who they were.

As soon as there is another person in the room, however, it is much more difficult to get to this experimental stage, because it is harder to stay clear from prejudices and preconceived views of the client's identity.

In Sam's case, music therapy could only work because the therapist managed not to take over other people's view of her and consequently their approach to her. Only by this means was it possible to offer Sam a different option for self-definition. However, there are many cases in which this does not work out as well. It is very easy to be biased by an assistant's views of, or feelings towards a client.

What is more, a client's behaviour will not be neutral either. A client's behaviour will be influenced by the attitude of people around him. This means that an assistant in the session who brings their own perceptions of the client, will inevitably have an influence on the client's behaviour, which will, in turn, have an impact on the therapist's view of the client, and make it even harder to keep a neutral, unprejudiced position.

Transference and countertransference

When collecting information on this subject in relation to assistants in music therapy sessions, I realised that while there is a lot of literature on transference issues, none of this mentions situations where there is an assistant present in the session.

My own approach to music therapy is largely person-centred, with an openness to other approaches and ideas. In the presence of an assistant, I will be highly unlikely to actively use a psychoanalytically informed approach – I might only bear its ideas in mind, and use them in order to try and understand a process. I would, however, never make the therapeutic relationship the centre of the conversation, while there is another person in the room. Therefore, I did not feel I could draw on case examples from my own clinical work, when discussing transference issues in relation to assistants in music therapy sessions.

I gained some information through personal conversations with four different music therapists who had said on the questionnaire that they usually worked in a psychoanalytically informed way and who occasionally worked with assistants in their sessions.

All four colleagues said that they tended to change their approach towards one that did not put the therapeutic relationship into the centre of the conversation, as soon as there was another person present. All four therapists said that they found the presence of an assistant to be extremely difficult because it forced them to take a different approach to the one they would usually have taken.

Two therapists said, however, that despite not talking about the therapeutic relationship in as great a depth as they would usually have done, psychoanalytically informed ideas did influence their thinking about the process a lot, which would in turn influence their decisions and their music.

This chapter is based on my own thoughts about transference issues in relation to assistants in music therapy sessions, taking music therapy literature on transference as a starting point. It is also based on the talks I had with colleagues about their own thoughts and experiences with transference issues in the presence of an assistant in the room.

Music therapy literature on transference and countertransference issues normally deals with transference and countertransference between the client and the therapist. A lot has been written about the various ways in which transference and countertransference can arise in a therapeutic context, about ways in which a therapist can actively work with a transference situation and make use of it in order to help the client gain some insight into their relationship patterns, feelings about people outside the therapy context, and feelings about past events or past relationships, especially relationships with previous primary caregivers.

Mary Priestley developed analytical music therapy and taught this approach in England and Germany. She wrote extensively about transference and countertransference matters in music therapy, discussing different kinds of transference and countertransference, how a music therapist can work with these and the role music plays. She put particular emphasis on the non-verbal nature of musical improvisation and on musical holding, which may resonate with a client's preverbal experiences and therefore bring about very strong transference (Priestley 1994). Other music therapists took up her ideas and developed them further. Kenneth E. Bruscia wrote about the therapeutic relationship, giving particular attention to transference and countertransference issues, including essays by other authors on transference matters in his book (Bruscia 1988). Johannes T. Eschen edited another collection of essays on analytical music therapy and on transference and countertransference issues in music therapy (Eschen 2002). Numerous other authors who have written on music therapy in relation to transference and countertransference include Diane Austin, Edith Lecaurt, Mechthild Langenberg, Benedikte B. Scheiby, David John, Helen Odell-Miller and Elaine Streeter.

However, none of the writings deal with situations in which there is a relationship other than the two way client- therapist relationship.

When there is another person in the room, transference issues may start to be a lot more complex and complicated. Now, there may be transference and countertransference not only between therapist and client, but now also between therapist and assistant, as well as between client and assistant. What's more – transference may arise between any one of those people in connection with the other two people together.

The assistant could transfer some of their own issues onto the therapist or vice versa. Trudy Klauber (in: Alvarez and Reid 1999: 39) describes cases where parents of autistic children, having suffered a lot of trauma relating to their child's diagnosis and treatment and their own dealings with insensitive professionals, suddenly vent their distress onto a current therapist. The therapist may become the target for feelings that actually belong to a past experience, and may experience hostility, feelings of abandonment (e.g. parents may suddenly start cancelling sessions), or defensiveness. Those feelings may seem inexplicable, unless the transference situation becomes apparent. They might also create countertransference in the therapist, which he or she may find hard to deal with such as anger, or disappointment, or a feeling of being let down, or a feeling of hurt pride. Such things could be triggered by something that reminds the parents of past trauma, for example, the therapist might become identified with this trauma through talking about diagnosis or history with the parents.

It is not difficult to imagine a situation in which this happens between an assistant and a music therapist or vice versa. An assistant could start to behave towards the music therapist as they would have behaved towards one of their own parents, or children, or other significant people in their lives whom the music therapist reminds them of. There might be something in the situation which triggers transference between the assistant and the therapist such as feelings of competition, or power issues, or a feeling of being taken care of, or a feeling that they have to take care of the music therapist.

Likewise, the therapist might unconsciously associate the assistant with a person outside the session. Sibling rivalry that has not been worked through may start to play a part, or some unfinished business with a parent may arise if the assistant is a lot older than the therapist.

Besides the added possibility of transference between assistant and music therapist, the transference situation will also change for the client. Now there is not just one person in relation to whom transference can arise, but two people. What's more – there is one person in the room with whom transference is bound to happen as part of the therapeutic process, and one person who the client knows from a different context and usually has a relationship outside the session with. Issues that are very real within this relationship and have to do only with the present and the assistant themselves will mix with transference issues that arise with the therapist.

The client could unconsciously make assumptions about the relationship between the assistant and the music therapist, for example, if the assistant was of about the client's age, and if the client felt that they would talk outside the session (while the client's contact with the therapist was restricted to a fifty- minute session per week), feelings of sibling rivalry could arise. This could, in turn, cause countertransference to arise in therapist or assistant or both, and this could influence their relationship with each other.

If the assistant was of a different gender from the music therapist, so that there was one male and one female person in the room, there could be an association with the client's parents and the client could transfer some of the issues he or she may have had with those onto the therapist and the assistant.

In light of this fact, it is not surprising that in most cases, transference and countertransference issues in the room will be far too complex to get a realistic grip of. The unravelling of transference and countertransference in the room could end in mere guess work.

An added complication arises because, while some therapists will actively work with transference that happens between client and themselves, and openly talk about it and work with it, this would be a highly unusual thing to do with transference issues arising that involved the assistant. This makes it much more difficult to acknowledge transference and use it as part of the therapy. Also, it means that not only is it harder, if not impossible, to use as a tool within the therapy process, but it is also harder to catch transference issues where they get into the way, i.e. if one person is struggling with the presence of another, or has feelings of anger or resentment.

The other difficulty is that, while it is not unusual to discuss the therapeutic relationship within the therapeutic boundaries, the presence of an assistant already changes the boundaries greatly, and the decision needs to be made again whether or not this approach is appropriate. The discussion of transference issues within the therapeutic relationship does require an extremely safe and protected space, and the presence of another person may seriously put this into question.

When transference arises between the therapist and the assistant, it must also be borne in mind that, in many cases, they will also have a relationship outside the therapy session, which complicates these matters even further. Transference matters will more easily mix with issues that clearly have to do with the present. This may make it even harder to get a grip on transference, if it arises.

Due to the fact that through the assistant's presence, the boundaries have shifted, it could be more appropriate for the therapist to just keep the possibility of arising transference in mind, but not to make it the centre of the conversation.

A problem that could arise when taking possible transference into consideration but, however, not discussing it as part of the therapy, and thus not checking assumptions against reality is the high risk of false guesses. When, for example, thinking about parental transference, the fact must be kept in mind that families do increasingly take forms other than the heterosexual two parent set up since children do grow up with a single parent, or with two legal parents of the same sex, or with one parent and other significant adults who participate in care and education. Jumping to the conclusion that 'family', for everybody, means one female and one male parent, would be too simple.

Many people actually stop talking about the therapeutic relationship as soon as there is an assistant in the session. However, even if this no longer forms the basis of what is being talked about in the session, transference and relationship matters are still around and usually an important factor in the progression of the therapy.

One colleague who I interviewed told me about the following case example and gave me permission to use it. My colleague worked with an assistant in a music therapy group, with the initial arrangement that she should be there all the time. With time, however, it turned out that she was repeatedly called by her manager to do other things during the time allocated to the music therapy group, so that sessions often had to be run without her. Although this was never actually a subject of discussion within the group, one client showed his anger about the assistant's repeated absence through his unconscious behaviour. He started criticising the assistant's music playing the next time she was present; then when the assistant stopped playing he criticised this as well. Although the therapist had not intended to particularly acknowledge or work with transference between the assistant and the clients, it struck the therapist that this client had had a very unreliable mother and that he had been moving in and out of care homes. When the therapist mentioned this observation to the client and asked whether there could have been a connection, there was a chance to acknowledge and talk through the client's feelings about his mother and how he felt about her having rejected him so many times.

The client then had a fresh experience with a female person in a caring role, since he felt he was taken seriously by the assistant. The assistant showed him that she felt his feelings to be valid both towards his mother as well as towards her absences in the group, when she had initially promised otherwise. Following a discussion in the group, the music therapist and the assistant had a talk with the manager and managed to change the situation, so that the assistant was finally able to come to the group more consistently. This also helped the client feel that this time, he had been taken seriously, that his feelings were valid and that there was a point in putting them into words, rather than swallowing them down. If the assistant had to stay away now, he was able to cope better. He had also learnt something for relationships with people around him. In this case, transference that arose between client and assistant actually became a valuable part of the therapy process.

It seems clear that, in many cases, transference and countertransference will arise, whether or not it is made the centre of the conversation in the therapy session. A. Gray makes the point that transference can arise in all kinds of relationships, not just in a therapy context (Gray 1994: 21). This means also that transference can arise not only in analytically informed music therapy, but in therapeutic situations of any approach.

The difference that the presence of an assistant can make is that in many situations, it will be more difficult, if not completely inappropriate, to openly address transference issues within the session. This, in turn, may easily cause transference issues to get into the way rather than being a vehicle towards therapeutic progress and insightful change.

The wish to prove oneself

Most of us will have experienced feelings of competitiveness, the need to prove our own role, or the fear of being judged by others. These feelings are very common, but we rarely openly admitted to them. It is also clear that, with an assistant present in the session, these feelings can grow much stronger.

The feelings can arise on both sides – on the side of the therapist or on the side of the assistant. And, although they are often not talked about openly, it is difficult not to let these feelings influence the work. They can impair decisions, the connection with one's own intuition, and can easily lead to an atmosphere of uneasiness in the room. Especially if the professional does not feel quite comfortable in the work setting, or feels under pressure to 'succeed' with some work, such feelings can seriously get in the way.

Most of the colleagues that I talked to said that they had felt under pressure to prove themselves, which was significantly stronger when there was an assistant in the room, especially if they were not sure of the assistant's attitude towards music therapy, or if they knew their attitude was negative or judgemental. It seemed to me that all of the people I spoke to had experienced this before, while only the degree and intensity of this seemed to vary.

One of the children I saw for a music therapy assessment was taken to the sessions by her nanny. The girl, Linda, was a fragile looking two and a half year old, who had only just been diagnosed as being "somewhere on the autistic spectrum". Especially since the only other child in the family, a brother of seven, had turned out to have Asperger's syndrome, the news of Linda's disability had rocked the family significantly. As yet, there was no clear information available, and the parents were still on a roller caster ride between hope and fear. There had not yet been sufficient time to deal with the second piece of traumatic news, and the family was quite obviously very tense and shaken up.

Linda's nanny Louise had been employed to live in with the family for five out of seven days of the week. When meeting her, it felt to me as if she had, in the midst of all this shock and emotional chaos, taken on quite a protective role and as if she was quite personally involved with the family situation.

Linda had always struggled with contact with strangers. This was part of what her diagnosis had been based on, and part of why she had been referred to music therapy. Linda had had to be taken out of preschool, because she had spent days crying. According to her files and according to her mother, Linda was able to make contact only with her parents as well as her nanny. All other strangers frightened her.

But it was not only Linda and Louise that brought some issues into the music therapy work. My own situation was also loaded with issues that had arisen in earlier work with the same employer.

When I had first started to work as a music therapist, I had been sent into a pre school group of autistic children. A number of things had gone wrong; and when I tried to deal with some negative feedback which my boss passed back on to me, communication broke down and there was no chance to improve the situation. Much as I tried taking some of the feedback on board, the opportunity group had already made up their mind and ended the music therapy contract for the end of the academic year.

Since the end of this particular work, I had not seen any other pre school children, and I felt an enormous pressure to prove that I could do this kind of work. This pressure was intensified due to the fact that Linda was one of the very few clients that I did not go to see in schools, but that she came to the building in which my colleagues worked. My pressure at around this time was so intense that at night I woke up with dreams about work.

The work started as terrifyingly as can be imagined for all people involved. Linda and Louise arrived, and Linda cried and screamed, did not want to come in through the door and clung to Louise's lap. The first session consisted of me talking to Louise and explaining about music therapy to her as if naming some of its benefits could make up for my feelings of helplessness in this situation.. Linda did not stop crying for the whole of the session. I tried singing, which did not help. I tried playing the guitar, but the appearance of the big instrument made Linda panic and curl up into Louise's lap just a bit more.

"She's always quiet instantly when I sing nursery rhymes to her", Louise said. "That's why we thought music therapy could do some good… you know…"

Likewise, the following session consisted of Linda crying and screaming and clinging to Louise's lap. I then suggested that Louise tried singing some of the nursery rhymes that she had said could calm Linda down.

"The wheels on the bus" and "If you're happy and you know it" had an immediate effect on Linda. She made eye contact with Louise, smiled and flirted with her.

It took several weeks to gradually find a way into the two-way relationship between Louise and Linda, by which time I had started secretly resenting Louise greatly. The pressure that I felt had also increased. I felt scared and resentful whenever Louise and Linda approached the music therapy building, with Linda screaming and crying loudly and audible to everybody in the building.

However, after a few sessions, there were slight signs of change.

Linda would not continue crying all through the session, but stop sooner and sooner. She would no longer cling to Louse's lap as fiercely, but sit up freely on her lap and eventually even sit by herself, next to Louise.

But, contrary to what I expected, this did not lead to a turning point or change to the situation. Whenever I felt I was just about to reach some point of connection with Linda, Louise did something to step in between Linda and me.

When Linda, for the first time, crawled off her lap and stopped crying so that she could listen to my guitar playing and quiet singing, Louise pulled her back onto her lap, and hissed "ssssh… don't be so scared".

Instantly, Linda started crying again.

"She doesn't like the guitar really", Louise said.

The same happened in the following session with the piano. I then took some big chime bars and let Louise play a slow, soft beat on a single note, while playing a melody on the xylophone and vocally reflecting back Linda's vocalisations.

This seemed fine and it looked as if I had managed to involve Louise and at the same time create some space for contact between

Linda and me. There were signs of development, first slight, then more clearly. Linda did not cry much at all now. She now sat in the middle of Louise and me. She made use of the three sounds she was able to make, and the tone and pitch of her vocalisations changed. They now sounded more confident and no longer terrified. Her body was erect and her eyes, even though she had not yet made eye contact with me, did examine the surroundings, showing a first slight sign of curiosity.

For my part, I was more than relieved that at least the crying had stopped, which had seemed to disqualify my abilities to be a music therapist, to anybody who could overhear from outside the room.

In the next session, I arranged the room in the same way before Linda and Louise arrived with the chime bar and beater ready for Louise, the xylophone ready for myself and some space for Linda to sit, in between these two instruments. It seemed to work. Then, suddenly, Linda openly gazed at me and vocalised back to me, picking up my pitch and speed.

At that same moment, Louise started singing "The wheels on the bus" in a loud voice, in a completely different pitch and key. The connection that had almost started to manifest itself between Linda and me had been aborted.

Nevertheless, the next session turned out be a good session, with some eye contact and vocal connection between Linda and me. The week after, however, Louise rang up and cancelled the session, because "Linda was upset today and would not be able to handle music therapy".

After that, each time that there had been a positive session with some connection between Linda and me, Louise cancelled the week after.

When I found out that Linda was going to attend the school in which I worked for one day per week, I decided to create a slot in which I would be able to see her. I felt that this would quite easily solve all the issues around this work. In addition, the family would no longer have to pay for music therapy nor take responsibility for getting her to her sessions.

I rang Linda's mother and suggested this new option to her. Linda's mother sounded pleased with the idea. There were going to be three more sessions in the old setting, before I was to start seeing Linda in school.

Linda did not turn up for her following session. When I rang her home number, Louise answered who told me Linda's brother had been sick and she had not been able to bring Linda. The other two sessions were also cancelled, for other reasons to do with Louse's workload.

Due to the family changing their mind about Linda's school placement, I never ended up seeing her again.

What had happened in this case? The relationship between myself and the assistant had seriously impaired the therapeutic relationship with the client, to an extent that music therapy work had become impossible. Both therapist and assistant had been under an enormous pressure to prove themselves, which had led to a situation of competition, in which therapist and assistant responded to each other rather than to the needs of the client. The relationship between the client and the therapist never really manifested, while the development of the work was determined by the relationship between therapist and assistant, and both their needs to prove themselves to each other, as well as to those people outside the room who were able to overhear.

While the carer managed to satisfy her wish to be more important and influential over the child than me, I, through being driven by my desire to prove myself, reached the opposite. Neither the carer nor myself were able to work towards the actual aims of the music therapy work, and to be helpful to the child.

This is an example of a situation in which music therapy work was impaired by the therapist's wish to prove herself.

Another issue, however, can be a music therapist's wish to convince other professionals or observers of the benefits of music therapy as a whole. This can be powerful, especially if the therapist is working in a surrounding where music therapy has not been long established, where it is still new and where not all the people involved have been in touch with it. The fact that issues around funding are often linked with other people's approval of the therapist and their work can add to this pressure significantly. Music therapy is, at present, a discipline which may be quite well established and accepted in a few places, but is still new and in its beginnings in many others. It is still a young discipline which, in many cases, needs to be approached with an attitude of promoting it and convincing others of its benefits

As opposed to a speech therapist or a physiotherapist, a music therapist may find himself or herself under greater pressure to justify their existence and convince others of the benefits of their job.

An added pressure can be the fact that a lot of music therapists work on a freelance basis and that their financial existence can hugely depend on the approval of the institution for which they work.

It has to be borne in mind that in many cases, there is not only a wish, but a very important need for the music therapist to prove themselves, which can be linked up with the survival of music therapy in a particular environment.

This wish or need to prove oneself or the value of music therapy can seriously get in the way, if, in order to reach approval, the therapist needs to collude with some dysfunctional behaviour patterns. In many cases, a problem could actually be rooted in the social context of the client, which could include the organisation itself which pays for music therapy. This could get the therapist into a situation of conflict. If they colluded with the dysfunctional social system, there may not be enough of a chance for the client to change. If the therapist does however choose not to encourage patterns that are unhealthy, they might lose their approval and possibly ultimately even their job.

During my work in a Special Needs School, I ran a group of four students in puberty age, which was sometimes joined by their class teacher, sometimes by a classroom assistant. One of the students had a tendency to display a lot of angry, challenging behaviour. He would do the opposite of what he was being told, he would not stay in his chair and would often actively try to disturb the rest of the group through playing the drum loudly when everybody else was playing quietly.

When talking to the teacher about his behaviour and her approach in class, the boy's angry attitude to school and to authorities became rather clear to me. It turned out that the student was good at drawing, and that he used this skill keenly and often. His drawings were collected in a big folder, which he treasured hugely. The teacher's way of disciplining him was to take control of the folder. She would take the folder off him at the beginning of a lesson, and every time that he did not comply with something, she would take a picture out of his collection and tear it up. The teacher advised me, in strong words, to take over the same strategy. She explained to me that the only way in which the student would comply with staff was through staff taking power over the folder of drawings, and through the threat of destroying one of them.

In the course of the same conversation, it also became clear that the boy had no real outlet for any of his feelings of anger, frustration or even just for the energy that a boy in the middle of puberty is bound to have.

I found myself in a difficult dilemma. At the time, this teacher was the only real supporter of music therapy in this school. Without her on my side, there was a realistic risk of losing the funding for music therapy through this school. On the other hand, it felt obvious to me that it was the teacher's strategy itself that fostered the large amount of challenging behaviour in the student.

I managed to deal with this issue through changing the set up of the group so that the teacher was as little involved with it as possible, and time tabled it so that the teacher had something else to do during this time and could no longer come in with the group, but left this task to a support assistant who would feed back to her after the session. I took the folder of drawings with me, but asked the student to show his drawings to me, and praised him for them. Then I placed the drawings on the piano, where they stayed for the rest of the session and all following sessions. I provided the student with big drums, which he could use to let off steam, and actively involved him as well as the other group members in decision making (which activities to pursue, in which moods, volume and on which instruments to play).

The situation did work out in the end, however this was only because I made some compromises that I did not feel comfortable about (by taking the folder of drawings into the session at all).

This kind of situation does, of course, require a lot of awareness of the conflict, careful balancing out of possibilities and constant judging of situations of dilemma.

Envy

Sometimes, the whole point of a music therapy case is the hope that the music therapist could reach a person who has not been reached by other professionals, who previously tried in other ways. It is often about connecting with people for whom language based methods of communication have not worked. A music therapist may often find themselves in a situation where they are required to try and connect with a person who has been impossible to reach by others involved in their care.

This is not only likely to increase the pressure the music therapist might feel towards the other professionals they are dealing with, who have referred the client or seen them referred by others, who are in communication with the music therapist about how their work with the client has been in the past and present. This situation has also got potential for feelings of threat or envy.

If the therapeutic relationship begins to work and if the therapist has managed to make a first step towards connecting with the client in musical ways, and then starts feeding this back to other professionals or carers, this might lead to feelings of comparison, possibly feelings of failure on their part.

Other things could give rise to envy. This could be differences in pay, differences in working conditions or personal responsibilities and social status.

Of course, feelings of envy could just as well arise the other way round, if, for example, a client manages to let off steam through taking part in sports activities but has not managed to do this through music therapy, or if speech and language therapy helps a child significantly more than music therapy.

In a normal work context, these feelings are to some extent not unusual, be it on the side of the music therapist or on the side of another professional. Normally, feelings of competitiveness or envy will occur in many work relationships and need not be a reason for concern or a serious hindrance to the work, if the professional is able to deal with their own feelings and does not let them get in the way of the work.

However, there are also situations where feelings of envy can impair a work relationship. This will become all the more powerful if these feelings govern a relationship between the music therapist and the assistant who is present during the music therapy work, and possibly the relationship with the client as well. This could lead to situations in which an assistant could unconsciously sabotage the work.

A colleague told me about a situation in which an assistant repeatedly 'forgot' the music therapy session, and took the client out on walks or school outings during the scheduled session time. Especially if there had been a session during which the contact between the music therapist and the client had made some progress, the next session was likely not to take place. Each time the assistant apologised to the therapist afterwards, promising that next time, she would remember the music therapy session; however, this never changed the situation.

When the music therapist did, however, share that she was about to quit her work in this particular school, and that the time that was left to work with this child was now limited, suddenly this problem ceased to exist. The assistant took care of the scheduled music therapy sessions and made sure that she and the client arrived on time.

My colleague felt that the issue had been the assistant's envy, and also, possibly, feelings of being threatened by the developing therapeutic relationship. Once it had become clear that she was going to leave, and therefore that this relationship was going to come to an end, there was no longer a basis for these feelings, and the assistant could change her unconscious behaviour.

3. Issues around the work setup

Boundaries and confidentiality

It is clear that boundaries have a very important function in a therapeutic relationship. However, with another person being present in the session, they will almost inevitably shift. Most music therapists stated on the questionnaire that they felt that boundaries had changed when they were working with assistants.

Probably the most affected area around boundaries this is confidentiality. Of course, some music therapy contexts will have a greater need for strict confidentiality boundaries than others. A psychoanalytically informed music therapy relationship, which takes place with a verbal adult in a mental health setting, will obviously need to be a lot stricter about boundaries and, especially, confidentiality. In a Special Needs school, where the emphasis is on music making with an autistic child and where there is no spoken language involved, this boundary might be a little bit looser.

However, confidentiality does remain an important issue when working with assistants. In a lot of cases, there will still be *some* exchange of words or personal information within the session, which needs a confidentiality boundary. Secondly, even non-verbal communication does qualify for confidentiality.

There are two different issues around confidentiality. The first one is the fact that the assistant themselves will be able to see and hear confidential information. The confidentiality boundary, therefore, has already been extended to include another person, who may or may not be a total stranger to the client. If assistants change, then there could be a whole number of different people, who will be able to hear and see different parts of the therapeutic process, and who will be able to hear and find out information which ought to be confidential.

The second issue concerns assistants talking about the session to other people, and passing on information.

Although, in theory, the assistant ought to be aware of confidentiality issues, and although the music therapist could remind the assistant of them, reality often shows that things are not the way they ought to be. A lot of the colleagues I talked to said they did not have enough time to talk to assistants, sometimes not enough opportunities to give them an idea even of the most basic points and ideas of music therapy. Sometimes, assistants will arrive together with the clients, and especially if a different assistant arrives with the client or group every time, it is difficult, if at all possible, to maintain communication.

Another issue is the question whether the client will still be able to perceive the session to be a 'safe space'. Even if the assistant knew about confidentiality boundaries, and there was good reason to believe that they would stick to them, the client's perception of the space and its boundaries would inevitably be a different one with another person in the room. The space would, inevitably, not feel as sheltered off from the rest of life.

It will be harder for the client to feel that they are completely free in talking about their lives, their environments and any feelings and issues connected with this. A lot of emotional issues will be connected with the client's environment, and therapy sometimes has to touch on this, if it wants to bring about any meaningful change. This is, of course, a lot more difficult to achieve if therapy cannot be a totally safe, neutral space, which is totally separate and sheltered from the rest of the client's life. Even if the music therapist has managed to ensure that the assistant will not talk to other people outside the session about what they have seen or heard in the session, the confidentiality boundary has still inevitably shifted, and this is very likely to have an impact on the therapeutic work

The degree of impact, which these issues have, will, of course, vary considerably depending on the context of the music therapy work. A music therapist working with children in a special school will face those questions less than a colleague who works with a highly verbal client in bereavement care.

Although music therapy literature does not mention this problem around confidentiality and assistants in sessions, this issue is being mentioned in connection with family members in play therapy sessions. Deborah and Donald McGuire (Mc Guire 2000: 42) talk about confidentiality in family therapy situations, and point out that anybody who works with more than one person in the room has got unique confidentiality concerns. The whole definition of boundaries, especially confidentiality boundaries, is more complex, needs clear addressing and needs taking seriously.

G. Corey goes even further in indicating that people who become involved in family therapy may have to relinquish some degree of confidentiality, as soon as there are more than two people in the therapy situation (Corey and Collanan 1988).

Another possible issue can be a clash between the boundaries a carer or assistant would set in their normal work context, and those that a therapist sets during their session. For example, a music therapist might pursue a particular approach to the client, while not realising that therapy actually supports or even encourages some behaviour that the carer, in a different context, had been working hard to stop or decrease. This might cause a serious clash.

A music therapist might choose a very non-directive approach to the client, which would shift boundaries in comparison to the client's other environments. The client might suddenly be allowed to do things that in other contexts would be unthinkable for them. The therapist might vocalise along with a client's screaming while the classroom assistant watching the session might have worked hard on decreasing the child's screaming in the classroom. Or the child might, in the session, be allowed to move around the room freely, which might cause a lot of discomfort to a teacher who had been working hard on getting the child to stay in his seat.

In this situation, it would not be surprising if the assistant felt their own efforts and achievements with the clients were being sabotaged, and felt that music therapy worked in a counterproductive way to what they themselves were doing. In this case, direct and mutually respectful communication will be needed, that will try to develop a common approach to the boundary question, and will seek to find a way forward which helps the child and can be supported by all professionals involved, as much as possible.

Clash of contexts

Clashes of therapeutic ideas with the reality of a particular work environment can be a difficult enough issue, even when the therapist is working by himself or herself. Many schools, hospitals or care homes have little understanding of some of the ideas that somebody thinking in psychotherapeutic terms may take for granted. They may not understand what the therapist is talking about when they ask for an undisturbed room, for reduction of noise outside the door, or when they try and explain why they cannot accompany the client on a school swimming trip.

On the other hand, somebody who had been trained only to think in psychotherapeutic ways, and wasn't flexible enough to try and understand other points of view, might find it hard to enter a dialogue that was effective enough.

These issues may become more difficult when assistants come into the therapist's sessions. The moment this happens, the therapist will have to negotiate therapeutic boundaries with those of the work context not only outside, but also inside the session.

An assistant may be used to taking up a completely different role from the one they are suddenly asked to play in the music therapy context. They may find that boundaries which, in the class room, they make great efforts to establish, suddenly don't exist during the music therapy session. A colleague told me of a situation in which she had improvised and sung along with her client's screaming and two noisy repetitive sounds. After a few weeks she was asked for a conversation with the head of the school, who told her that music therapy had been perceived to be counterproductive to efforts class had made with this pupil. It turned out that the music therapist had encouraged those very sounds in the client that teachers had been trying hard to decrease and discourage, because the boy's noises had been felt to be very disruptive to the other children.

Another example is a situation in which a group of children is allowed to freely move around the room, pick up and play whichever instruments they choose - or no instrument at all if they prefer. This may seriously clash with their teacher's approach, if they were trying to train students to sit still, listen to the teacher and do only as told.

Great difficulties might arise if the assistant is requested to take different roles in different settings - if, for example, they are asked to be very directive in a classroom context, but requested to hold back and allow the client to scream, walk around and take the lead in a music therapy context. They might feel that their own work was being devalued or even sabotaged, or they might simply find it very difficult to switch from one type of behaviour to another.

Likewise, this situation could create some serious confusion on the part of the client when the third person takes several roles and suddenly behaves in quite a different way from how they expect.

One of my groups was run with the help of a teacher, who was very supportive of music therapy, very understanding of its approach and ideas and very enthusiastic about helping it work in her school. Jeanette was a skilled oboist and took a musically active role within the session. Generally, we improvised together with the three highly autistic four year old boys and followed each other as well as the flow of the session, picking up the children's vocalisations, giving the pupils an outlet for their emotions and trying to contain them musically, reflecting their emotions back musically, etc. etc. The teacher had, in the past, had an interest in training to be a music therapist herself, although life had then taken her a different way. However, her role was very much that of co- therapist. Jeanette had, and made use of, improvisation skills. She made use of music by following her pupils through playing music and containing and matching their emotional expressions musically.

Although it felt, in many ways, as if the situation could not be better, it soon became apparent that there was a clash between her role in the music therapy sessions with me, and her role as a teacher in class.

In class, she would tell her pupils what to do, and take the lead. In the session, it was suddenly the children who took the lead, and who were being followed and musically contained by Jeanette and me. In class, the children were not allowed to scream, or to vocalise loudly, while in music therapy, this would be taken as a means of self expression, and integrated into the music.

One day, Jeanette arrived with two of the three boys, saying that this day had been particularly difficult so far. All three boys were a bit stirred up and upset on that day. She had not wanted to bring over all three boys at the same time. Therefore she left me with the two children and went back to class to pick up the remaining one. The boys were very stirred up indeed. Both of them would not sit in their seats, but ran around the room, crying and screaming, not being reached by words. Then, one of the boys picked up the bin from the corner behind the door, turned it upside down and started banging it like a drum. Feeling that there wasn't much I could do to get the boys to sit in their chairs or follow any activity, I just made sure that the bin was empty, then went to the piano and played along with this boy's bin- drum- playing. Within a few minutes, the boy and I had formed some connection, and he allowed me to musically be with him. Also, I managed to join the other boy's vocalisations, and I felt that although I had not been able to get the boys to be disciplined, sit down or be able to listen, there was some kind of connection within the chaos, some way of reaching the boys within the atmosphere of confusion.

As soon as the door opened and Jeanette came back in, however, the boy dropped the bin as fast as he could and made a quick escape to the other side of the room. For the rest of the session, neither Jeanette nor I managed to build a connection with any of the boys, engage them into an activity or get them to respond.

In this case, there had been a clear clash between Jeanette's role as a teacher and her role as a co- music therapist. Although she had not said or done anything to discourage her pupil from using the bin as a drum, he knew very well that in class, this would not have been acceptable. The boundaries, and the boundary difference between class and music therapy session, had been confusing.

Another issue is that normally a music therapy session tries to offer a non-judgemental space - while school is a context in which the pupil is much more likely to be judged. This might throw the assistant's role (and the client's perception of it) into a conflict. What, for example, if the assistant's task is to support behaviour management? This will mean that there is a clear judgemental presence in the room - more so, a person who is present for no other reason than to monitor and judge. The client is likely to find it harder to express their feelings openly and directly.

Also, the clash of context can involve great challenges for the carer. Music therapy may well involve something which they do not know, find strange, fear, or find very difficult. It may involve something which goes against the assistant's beliefs or against what they are working towards themselves.

Especially because music therapy is often about emotions and about their expression, this may easily touch on something that the assistant may find difficult, if the emotion that is being expressed is not within the range of socially accepted feelings, such as joy, fun, or happiness. A carer might want the client to express their emotions, but at the same time they might want them only to express *some* emotions - but not others. They might find it very hard to handle if that involves the expression of anger, sadness or fear.

It might also be the case that the assistant experiences the client being allowed to express something which they have always had to suppress in themselves, such as the expression of anger. This could make it very hard to tolerate.

Thirteen music therapists stated on the questionnaire that the relationship between themselves and the work setting had been influenced by an assistant's presence. However, only some of them said this influence was a negative one. Several music therapists who I spoke to about this issue said that they felt that in the long run, the relationship improved, because the assistant could also act as a bridge between the two different settings. The clash could be something that could be worked with, and approached with an attitude of openness and communication. In talks with colleagues, I found that this generally worked better where there was a greater understanding of music therapy in the work setting.

Interestingly enough, none of the assistants I interviewed said that they found the differences in context difficult. This did, at first, seem surprising, given the fact that from my own experience, clashes in context seems to often be an issue, and given the fact that a lot of my music therapy colleagues also perceived these clashes to be a common problem.

However, when thinking about assistant feedback more, I felt this could be explained by the fact that those assistants who filled in the questionnaire / volunteered to be interviewed about their experiences in the first place may be those who approach music therapy with a certain degree of openness anyway. As such, the interviews with assistants are, of course, no fully representative source. I am still inclined to think that the issue of context differences and context clashes is a very major one when working with assistants in music therapy sessions.

4. Issues around the therapy process

The luxury of not knowing

Working as a professional person, with an audience in the same room can increase the pressure on the therapist to 'know' the road all the time, to have answers and readily available methods to deal with any situation that could arise.

In a lot of situations, the therapist will need to draw on their professional knowledge and inner road maps of music therapy. In many cases, it is useful to have vast knowledge of music therapy theory, of different diagnostic tools and of approaches other therapists have tried out and written about.

Sometimes, however, great value can lie in moments of openness, of not exactly knowing where the path will lead, of what is going to happen next. Much as it is important for a music therapist to be able to draw on enough pre- acquired knowledge about his or her tools, it can be just as valuable to be able to drop and question those tools and preconceived information for moments, when appropriate.

Sometimes a moment of uncertainty can create valuable momentum. If the therapist can, in a situation of ambivalence or of not being sure, resist the temptation to find safety in a preconceived idea or in a tried and tested method, then this could create valuable momentum, allowing a connection with the client and with the current situation on a much deeper level and could lead to answers that are much more honest and insightful. The risk of pigeon holing a person or a situation may then be avoided. It may also prevent the therapist from losing a feel for the client as an individual, with his or her very own needs and with his very own personality, and of making assumptions or forming judgements too quickly.

It is important to find a good balance between drawing on one's own pre-achieved background knowledge, and being able to let go of one's professional road map at times, questioning it, and allowing for some openness to changing it.

It is, however, harder – and at times impossible – to allow for this openness and, sometimes, inevitable lack of security that goes along with this, when there is an audience present in the room; especially when the presence of the third person is felt to be judgemental. A greater challenge is then presented to the therapist to allow for moments of openness and, when appropriate, to drop the role of the 'knowledgeable professional' for a moment.

Sixteen music therapists stated on the questionnaire that they felt an assistant's presence could impair their willingness to take risks or be open to the yet unknown. Only one music therapist said that this was never at all an issue.

The fine balance between hope, expectations and unconditional acceptance

Therapy often seems to work with a paradox that a therapist has to negotiate. Various people have pointed out that a certain attitude of hope for change is actually an important part of the therapist's attitude towards the client. On the other hand, there is also the need for unconditional respect for the client's own choices.

How does one convey to the client that there is unconditional regard and acceptance, when on the other hand, the very reason the client is in therapy is bound up with the notion that he or she should change?

This dilemma does come up time and again in discussion about therapeutic work and approaches. Therapy needs to negotiate this paradox again and again, in particular when the client is someone who has not themselves chosen to be in therapy. Karin Schumacher points out that an important precondition of the work with autistic children is an attitude of hope for contact in the future, while at the same time, if this leads to an expectation or claim of contact, this might cause the child to withdraw (Schumacher 1994: 10). Schumacher acknowledges that this is a very tricky dilemma to negotiate.

Also, the music therapist will need to deal with feelings on their own part that will be triggered by this process. If they approach the client with an attitude of hope, then it can be difficult not to get attached to the wish for contact or positive change in the client, and it may be necessary to deal with feelings of frustration, disappointment, rejection or self doubt. At the same time, it will be necessary to continue music therapy work with the same attitude of hope and non-forcefulness, not letting feelings of frustration get into the way and not giving up on the client.

What is the impact the presence of an assistant could have on all this?

The presence of an audience could make this conflict more intense, and cause the dilemmas in this situation to be harder to negotiate. This can be due to the following reasons.

An assistant will bring their very own attitudes, hopes, expectations and also disappointments with them. They will have had a history with this client, which has formed their attitude. They may want the therapist to have an instant success, or even expect them to perform a miracle; or they may not wish this to happen, because it may feel like a threat to their own hard work with the client.

Another issue is that the music therapist might feel under more of an unspoken pressure to succeed, which may make it a lot harder to get the balance right. It could make it harder for the music therapist to resist trying to push the client.

Or the assistant might have personal feelings about the client and feel strongly judgemental about some aspects of his or her person or behaviour. This could make it a lot harder for the music therapist to create an atmosphere of unconditional acceptance and non-judgementalism.

All these things will add complications to the dynamics and intensify the need for balance between the hope for change and unconditional acceptance of the client.

Another issue is the potential for clash between different people's hopes and expectations. Even in a therapeutic situation which does not involve the presence of another person in the room, there can be a clash between the therapist's hope or expectation of where the work would lead, and the client's. Normally, this situation would require very clear communication, at the beginning of the work and, as needed, throughout the process. When there is an assistant present, this issue can become even stronger. Now, it is not only the therapist and the client who need to match their hopes and expectations of where the process would lead, but the assistant will bring their own ones as well.

An example for this is a clash of expectations between myself and a teacher, who referred one of her students to me. The teenage boy had been extremely difficult in class, had been displaying a lot of challenging behaviour and outbursts of anger, which led him to scream, throw himself onto the floor, hit other children and himself, and which disrupted his own as well as the learning process of children around him.

When I started working with Jake, the road forward soon seemed to be fairly clear to me. The aim which I had soon decided I would pursue for Jake was to give him an outlet for all his surplus energy, a safe space where he could express any of his feelings, and a chance to learn how to channel the expression of his feelings, so that he could choose between appropriate and inappropriate ways of doing so.

I therefore let him play loud music on the drums if he so chose, accompanying him on the piano, and put the focus on showing him that there were different ways of expressing emotion and that it was acceptable to play wild music, but not to throw the beaters across the room or hit the assistant who came to bring him to the session.

In feedback talks with the teacher, however, it soon turned out that her expectations had been very different. The teacher expressed some concern in the fact that we were playing loud music, if, as she put it, the whole point of music therapy was to get him to be quiet. She asked me if I couldn't play some calm relaxation music to him and get him to stop his tantrums this way. In her mind, my role was to find I way that I could stop any angry emotions and any energy outbursts in Jake, and to transform him to a quiet boy who was always happy.

In this case, as in many others, the solution to this issue was clear communication, which had failed in the beginning. I explained more clearly to the teacher what music therapy was about, in which ways it could help and what I could and couldn't do. In this case, the situation worked out okay in the end. The teacher agreed to try music therapy with Jake a little longer, to see whether it would benefit him. I worked with him for another year, during which I felt supported by the teacher and during which we both observed some progress in Jake's behaviour in class and towards peers.

In their book on play therapy and dealing with client's parents, Deborah and Donald McGuire write about possible clashes between parents' and therapist's expectations of goals for the therapy work, and about the need for clear communication, where possible right from the start[1]. Although this book does not address work with assistants, I feel that the same issue can also arise when dealing with assistants.

In all of those cases, it seems clear that major importance lies in communication between the assistant, the therapist and (where

---

[1] Mc Guire, Deborah and Donald: Linking Parents to Play Therapy. p. 10

possible) the client. The other thing that has crucial importance is the therapist's reflection on their own goals, hopes and expectations.

Whose norms? Whose limits?

One thought that I found myself increasingly confronted with as clients of mine started offering me glimpses into their worlds, into their life concepts and into what did or did not make sense to them, was the question of norm, of social expectations and social rules.

Is it really only the case that those people we are working with fail to fit into our ideas of how a person should be, how they should behave, how they should think and feel, what they should like or dislike or could this not also be looked at in the reverse? Is it not equally the case that 'normal', i.e. non-disabled, people have a range of preconceived ideas, obsessions and limiting views and explanations of the world? Could it not sometimes be true that a disabled, or simply 'different', person simply does not share the same preconceptions and fixed views and that this might greatly contribute to the difficulties some disabled people may have in connecting with a social context of non-disabled people?

This clash of norms and preconceptions can be one of the greatest fascinations of being a music therapist. It can feel extremely inspiring, often challenging and often liberating, to be forced to escape our own world of thinking and perceiving, of social norms and ways of making and cultivating contact, and to go to new concepts of all this. This can make contact with disabled people so challenging, rich and liberating.

As a music therapist, I do have a safe and rather privileged role when it comes to experiencing all the fascinating and interesting parts of somebody else's world. Usually, there is a safe, contained space along with an unconventional medium of contact, which offers great potential for exploration, for discovery and for new forms of experience but without the cost of losing status or contact with the outside world.

As a music therapist, I can join in with my client's vocalisations; I can howl or bark like a dog and sit on the floor with them; I can play hide and seek with a curtain or roll a rain stick back and forth, joining a client's game that pretends it is a locomotive. At the same time, I do not lose status and social acceptance for doing all these things.

As such, a music therapist has a double role. The music therapist's role is that of a bridge, sometimes a negotiator between different norms.

The question that arises – and never ceases to need negotiation – is to what extent the client should be encouraged, enabled or sometimes forced to join norms of the outside world. Most people would agree that it is a good idea to teach an adult not to blow their nose on the tablecloth. On the other hand, should a person be discouraged from saying "ra galata ta" all day, if for them, this is a valid method of self-expression and communication?

Being a music therapist to people with learning disabilities involves constantly learning about the personal norms and perceptions of the clients, as well as those of the people, maybe institutions around them and negotiating the differences while making sure that the therapist's own norms and preconceptions don't get in the way of this. This requires constant openness, constant questioning, constant negotiation and a constant making oneself aware of one's own concepts and ideas of good and bad.

So what then is the impact that a visitor or an observer in a music therapy session can have on this question of negotiation?

First of all, this does of course depend on which role the assistant has within the sessions. The assistant could be merely an observer, or he or she could be actively participating.

If the assistant were merely an observer, they would be less likely to give up any of their own norms and concepts. This would make it harder for the therapist to have a completely neutral and unbiased role. It could be that an assistant made the therapist more self conscious, and slightly less willing to take risks towards exploring the client's world, their norms and ways of behaving. An extra person's presence might keep the therapist from diving into the client's world quite so freely, and doing things that an outsider might regard as odd. The therapist might be less likely to connect with the client through playfully making animal noises at each other, or joining the client in rolling herself around on the floor, or playing hide and seek. The balance might tip slightly more towards the norms of the outside world and the ways in which the music therapist wishes to be seen within those norms.

The presence of an assistant might, of course, have more of an impact in this way, the more critical the therapist feels the assistant to be. If the therapist perceives the assistant to be positive towards whatever they are doing, it may be easier to take a risk. If the assistant is felt to be a critical presence, it may be a lot harder for the therapist to remain uninfluenced.

On the other hand, an assistant could also help foster the bridge between the client's norms and the norms of the social context of the client. They could offer valuable explanations about behaviours.

In some cases, the assistant might even join in exploring the client's personal norms and perceptions. They might join in a playful interaction that is sparked off by a client's particular way of behaving, or they might join in a piece of music that is based on some sound or vocalisation of the client. They might be open to watching something that happens in the music therapy session and thinking it through together with the therapist, reflecting together with the therapist about the client's behaviour and what makes sense to them or not, and why. They might offer valuable suggestions both about the therapy session as well as about the client's surroundings outside the session. As such, they may assist the therapist in being a bridge, making use of the fact that they often have closer links with the client's world outside the session than the therapist does.

In a group which I ran for three adults with mild learning difficulties in their home, I found myself confronted with those questions around norms and how to negotiate between a group of clients' norms and those of the outside world.

One of my main aims was to give these three people an experience of taking full responsibility for themselves, of being adults in a world which often tends to treat them as children, to give them an experience of a context in which they were not been spoon- fed or asked to comply, but in which there was some space for their own choices, expression of emotions or thoughts.

I therefore had an attitude of being as little directive as the situation could possibly afford. I risked not making suggestions, and I risked moments of silence. My aim was just to be encouraging and positive towards any kind of initiative from the three clients. Gradually, all three group members moved to a stage where they were increasingly able to voice their wishes, suggest ideas and suggest what they did or did not want to do.

However, I did feel concerned by the fact that one favourite choice was the song 'Bah bah black sheep'. One fifty year old lady especially delighted in this choice over and over again and eventually even managed to take the lead while strumming the guitar, at the same time growing in confidence and expressiveness while singing this song which she knew and loved.

But was it really appropriate for a group of adults to be singing a nursery rhyme, if the whole idea of the group was to help three people behave like adults?

After a lot of reflection and a discussion with my supervisor, I decided that if I was being honest and consistent with my idea about treating the three group members as responsible adults, then who was I to decide for them that 'Bah bah black sheep' was not an appropriate song to sing? If I decided which music was right for which person or purpose, wasn't that actually a consequence of my own preconceived view that I had adapted because I had been part of a social context that runs on limiting beliefs and narrow views?

In due course, I let my clients sing and enjoy 'Bah bah black sheep', if they so chose, (however, admittedly being glad that I was not running this group with an assistant from the home), while at the same time making sure that I introduced a range of other songs as well, to offer them a bigger choice and make them aware of more different kinds of music that existed as well as nursery rhymes.

When I arrived at the home for the last time before the summer break, there had been a little bit of confusion around my session. Staff had planned a garden party for the residents, and they had forgotten to ring me and cancel the music therapy session. The party had already started, and it was apparent enough that my three clients were having a good time and would not have wanted to be removed from this situation.

The home manager then suggested that we simply turned the garden party into a concert, and that my clients and I performed some of the music that we had been doing. I asked the three people, and they all agreed enthusiastically. We went into the house to choose some songs that we could perform, and I asked each of the clients to suggest what they would most like to sing.

The first idea, keenly spoken, was 'Bah bah black sheep'. But at this point I lost my courage. I suggested that we chose something else, which subsequently happened, so that staff and fellow residents never got to hear the nursery rhyme performed by the group.

What had happened here?

I had got myself into two conflicting social norms. My cultural background suggested that nursery rhymes should only be sung by or for children. However, the group built up a norm that was different from this. This norm, which made perfect sense, was that all music is appropriate, if adults choose it freely and enjoy it. I had no problem accepting this new norm after a little bit of reflection, as long as the group was a self contained space that was separate from the outside world.

The moment our music was supposed to be performed to an audience (more so – an audience that actually paid me for running this group), I backed out and betrayed the group of their freedom to make a responsible choice for themselves. Instead of creating a bridge between two different sets of norms, I saw myself in a dilemma which at this moment (and taken by surprise) I could only solve through suppressing the group's norm.

Had the group permanently involved an assistant, then the whole process of forming a norm could have been a different one. It could have been that the group had adapted to the norm the assistant would have regarded as normal. Likewise, it could have been that the assistant had adapted and accepted the new norm of the group, or helped in the process of creating a bridge.

5. Working through, working with or working to minimise?

As we have seen, there are two different choices the music therapist can make, if he or she works with an assistant in the session.

The first possibility is to try and minimise the assistant's input and influence. This could be done by asking the person not to contribute, or to contribute only as little as possible, by getting the person to step back and have as little influence on the therapeutic dynamics as possible. The danger here, of course, is that it would then be easy to fall into the trap of believing that the therapeutic process could enfold as if there were only two people in the room. However, it is important not to deny the fact that the assistant, even if their role is very held back, is inevitably going to have an influence on the session, on the relationship and on the therapeutic process.

The other option is to actively involve the assistant in the therapeutic process, and work towards making them an acknowledged part of the sessions and therapeutic relationship. This would mean looking at any issues that arise out of the presence of the assistant, acknowledging them as part of the session, and trying to work with them. If a conscious choice is made that the assistant is an active part of the dynamics, then issues around their presence could be regarded as part of the therapeutic process and dynamics.

Potential difficulties could arise here, as we have seen in previous chapters. Those problems could arise if issues around the assistant's presence cannot be worked through (e.g. if their role cannot be appropriately clarified), if issues between the assistant and the client cannot be worked through (such as a fixed negative view of the client), if personal feelings between assistant and therapist (such as envy, rivalry, the fear of being judged, transference issues or fixed preconceived views) become the focus of the session, if the assistant does not have enough of an understanding of therapy and its boundaries, if there is not enough time and opportunity to communicate with the assistant, if clashes between the assistant's work context and the therapy session cannot be worked with, or if, for any other reason, the main focus ceases to be on the client and their needs.

In order to illustrate this, I would like to recall some of the case examples I wrote about earlier, and look at them in the light of this question.

In chapter 2, I talked about the girl Emma, who claimed her care assistant's attention by repeatedly throwing the lid of her breathing tube onto the floor. In this case, the assistant and I had tried to create a situation which pretended that there was only a two way relationship - through me asking the assistant to step back and not take up a role within the therapeutic relationship. However, Emma forced the assistant back into the dynamics, and, in so doing, taught me that the assistant's presence cannot be without an influence on the session. Here is an example of a situation which pointed to the fact that, even if the therapist chooses to follow the first option and make the assistant step back, it is impossible to create a situation in which the assistant has no role at all - as long as the assistant is still in the room.

The other case example which I wrote about in this chapter, leads to the same conclusion. My colleague, who worked with a potentially violent man and his support worker in the session, tried to get the assistant to make herself as unobtrusive as possible, by asking her to look out of the window or to bring a book to read. This, however, caused the client to try to get his support worker's attention more and more, and eventually it resulted in him hitting a drum so hard that it broke.

Those are just two examples that highlight the fact that an assistant will always be part of the dynamics no matter whether or not they try to hold back and try to keep out of the dynamics. The conclusion to be drawn from this is that the therapist, even if they choose to get the assistant to step back as much as possible, has to acknowledge the fact that their presence will still have some influence on the therapy work.

However, it is also clear that asking the assistant to step back can still be the most appropriate choice to make. This applies to situations in which it is not possible to work through issues that arise out of the assistant's presence, and make them a valid part of the therapy work, rather than a stumbling block or something which holds back the process.

I have mentioned situations in which music therapists had to intervene when an assistant took a client's hand and made them play an instrument, assuming that their role involved making the client play an instrument as much as possible. In such cases, it is necessary for the music therapist to get the assistant to step back a little.

In chapter 2, I also talked about the girl Sam, whose relationship with her care assistant got in the way of the therapy work, in that the assistant's fear of and disillusionment with Sam's challenging behaviour triggered the very behaviour which the assistant's presence had been seeking to avoid. In this case, the only possible way to enable good therapy work to take place, was to get the assistant to step back and sit next to the door, not actually in the room.

These are examples where the best choice turned out to be to try and make the assistant decrease their input and influence, and try and give them as little a role within the therapeutic relationship as possible.

Now, I will look at a few case examples where the other strategy has been applied - where the assistant is considered to be a part of the therapeutic process and relationship, and where this is consciously worked with.

In chapter 2, I wrote about a support assistant's involvement with a group, who told one of the boys to 'behave himself and be happy'. Although this remark of hers was, at the very moment that it was made, not particularly helpful to the boy nor to the music therapy situation, it did cause a helpful revelation. It brought a problem to light which was present in the boy's environment. Although I was unable to change the boy's environment, I was, however, able to understand the boy and his behaviour better than I would otherwise have, and the assistant's comment and the information it subsequently revealed did enable me to respond to this boy more appropriately in the future. In particular, I was able to make sure that I could give him even more outlets for his emotions, which he had no chance of expressing outside of the session.

In this case, it turned out that the assistant's presence, and large involvement with the group and the group process, played a significant positive part. More so, it turned out that an issue that was caused by her presence could actually be treated as part of the therapeutic process, and play a part in it.

Chapter 3 mentions my colleague's music therapy group, in which a client felt upset by the fact that the assistant could repeatedly not come to the music therapy group. When those feelings were treated as a valid part of the music therapy work, the client's feelings acknowledged and taken seriously and the transference situation also acknowledged, this could move the music therapy work on in a productive way. It enabled the client to understand something about himself, and even enabled him to have a corrective experience. This is another case example illustrating a situation where the assistant played a full part in the group process, and where an issue arising out of her relationship with a client could be used to give the client some insight, the experience of being taken seriously and the experience of a different kind of conflict resolution.

In some cases, there may be issues around the assistant's presence, which can be resolved through neither option. There may be situations when it is neither helpful to get the assistant to step back, nor to work through issues as part of the therapy. In such a case, it might not be possible to continue the work with a particular assistant at all.

I wrote about two examples where this was the case, the first one concerned Louise and Linda, where competition between me and the assistant got so strong that it prevented a relationship between me and the client to develop, and the second one concerning the teacher who pressurised me to tear up her pupil's drawings in cases where he displayed any angry emotion.

In those cases, music therapy work with a particular assistant in the session turned out to be impossible, because it was possible neither to work through the issues that had arisen as part of the therapy process, nor to get the assistant to minimise their input so that the issues did not get in the way of the therapy process.

If the assistant's presence can be positively integrated into the music therapy work, then the extra person can be a valuable source of information about the client in a different context, about the previous days or week, or about the client's life. The assistant can be a bridge between therapy and the outer world. Their presence can foster dialogue or make at least make communication a lot easier. If their presence can be acknowledged to be a part of the session and worked with as part of the process, then this can open doors to make the work a lot richer and a lot more insightful.

Whatever choice the music therapist makes, it is clear that the assistant will always have an impact on the therapeutic process, and that this will be the case whether or not the music therapist chooses to actively involve them into conversation and music making, or not.

The question to ask is, therefore, not *whether*, but rather *what kind of* influence an assistant's presence has on a music therapy session, and which issues this can raise and which choices the music therapist has for responding to them.

It is empowering to consider the dynamics between the assistant, the client and the therapist instead of only thinking about the dynamics between the client and the therapist. If we choose to do this, then we can make conscious choices about the situation, about what we say and do, about playing music and about how we support the therapeutic process. It also allows us to continue to improve communication with assistants as well as with all the other people involved.

And finally, it can keep us from falling into the trap of pretending that the situation is something that it cannot be: A safe, undisturbed, two-way therapeutic relationship. Instead, it can give us the opportunity to work with the situation as it really is and to try and acknowledge and integrate the assistant's presence into the therapeutic process.

German summary/Deutsche Zusammenfassung

Peter ist erschöpft. Fünfundzwanzig Minuten lang hat er mit aller Kraft zwei riesige aufeinandergestapelte Trommeln bearbeitet und, zusammen mit meinem lebhaften, aber rhythmisch strukturierten Klavierspiel, laute Rufe von sich gegeben.

Peter, ein siebzehnjähriger junger Mann mit Down-Syndrom, ist mir in die Musiktherapie überwiesen worden, weil sein aggressives Verhalten für seine Klasse kaum mehr tragbar gewesen ist. Jetzt lernt er allmählich, daß Energie und Emotion zwar nicht „böse" sind, daß man diese aber mitunter kanalisieren muß und daß es gute und schlechte Arten gibt, mit manchen Emotionen umzugehen. Die Arbeit mit Peter gestaltet sich sehr befriedigend. Unsere gemeinsame Musik ist inspiriert und inspirierend, energiegeladen und reich an unterschiedlichsten Farben und emotionalen Momenten. Seit Peter mit der Musiktherapie begonnen hat, ist sein aggressives Verhalten in der Klasse zurückgegangen.

Obwohl in der Musiktherapie noch nie eine kritische oder gefährliche Situation entstanden ist, war dennoch von Anfang an klar, daß ich mit dem kräftigen, zu Wutanfällen neigenden, mitunter auch körperlich aggressiven jungen Mann nicht alleine im Raum sein kann. Deshalb erscheint Peter jede Woche zusammen mit einer Assistentin, einer kräftigen Dame mittleren Alters, die sowohl Peter als auch mir gegenüber eine mütterliche Rolle einnimmt. In der

Regel setzt sie sich in eine Ecke, nickt mir freundlich zu und beschränkt sich darauf, aus wachen, warmen Augen das Geschehen zu beobachten.

Jetzt hat Peter sich müde gespielt. Mit einem erschöpften und zufriedenen Lächeln rollt er sich auf dem Fußboden zusammen und schaut zu mir am Klavier hinüber. Was folgt, ist ein Moment von gemeinsamer Stille, die ein Schlüsselmoment in unserer bisherigen Arbeit zu sein scheint: wir können zusammen Musik machen, laut und wild sein, doch wir können auch zusammen schweigen und dabei in Kontakt bleiben. Ob Peter schon einmal mit anderen Menschen auf diese neue, stille Art Kontakt aufgenommen hat?

In diesem Moment erhebt sich die Assistentin von ihrem Stuhl.

„Ich sehe gerade, daß er nicht beschäftigt ist", sagt sie. „Ich wollte Ihnen doch noch die Fotos von meinem Enkelsohn zeigen... jetzt wär' doch gerade ein guter Moment...?"

Vieles ist geschrieben worden über die Beziehung zwischen Musiktherapeut und Klient, über die Rolle der Musik innerhalb dieser Beziehung, über Übertragung und Gegenübertragung. Fast jeder Winkel dieser therapeutischen Beziehung ist ausgeleuchtet worden. Doch was, wenn diese Beziehung eine dritte Person mit einschließt? Eine Person, die unweigerlich ein Teil des Geschehens im Raum ist – aber dennoch weder Therapeut noch Klient? Eine Person, die ganz eigene zwischenmenschliche und therapeutische Prozesse in Gang setzt?

Doch welche zusätzlichen Dynamiken sind das, die da in Gang kommen können? Und wie geht man mit ihnen um? Wie verändert sich der therapeutische Prozeß, die therapeutische Beziehung, wie verändern sich die Rahmenbedingungen der Musiktherapie, die man möglicherweise immer für völlig selbstverständlich gehalten hat?

Meine Arbeit an diesem Thema begann, als ich für meine MA-Diplomarbeit an der APU Cambridge ausführliche Recherchen anstellte. Ich sprach mit Kollegen über ihre Erfahrungen zu diesem Thema, befragte Assistenten zu ihrer Perspektive und sammelte Ergebnisse durch Fragebögen. Mittlerweile kann ich diese Ergebnisse durch meine siebenjährige Berufserfahrung als Musiktherapeutin ergänzen.

Je mehr ich mich mit diesem Thema befaßte, desto deutlicher wurde, daß viele der Fragen, Herausforderungen und Probleme um dieses Thema mit einer Kernfrage zusammenhängen – der Frage nämlich, welche Rolle man dem Assistenten innerhalb des musiktherapeutischen Geschehen zuweist, und welche Konsequenzen für den jeweiligen Prozeß diese Entscheidung hat.

Eine zweite Kernfrage, die sich aufdrängt, ist, ob der Assistent eigentlich als Teil des therapeutischen Prozesses betrachtet werden sollte oder nicht. Die Antwort darauf hängt natürlich wiederum mit der ersten Frage zusammen, und auch aus ihr ergeben sich wiederum verschiedene Konsequenzen für die therapeutische Arbeit. Darauf werde ich später noch einmal zurückkommen.

Etwa ein Drittel der Musiktherapiekollegen, die meinen Fragebogen ausfüllten, kreuzten an, daß sie Assistenten in der Regel als Teil des therapeutischen Prozesses betrachten. Ein weiteres Drittel gab an, daß sie Assistenten eher als außerhalb dieses Prozesses stehend sahen. Die übrigen Kollegen wählten die Angabe, dies variiere von Fall zu Fall.

Deutlich wurde auch, daß die Entscheidungen, auf welche Rolle hingearbeitet wurde, sehr unterschiedlich ausfielen. Manche Kollegen sagten, ihnen sei es am liebsten, wenn der Assistent so unauffällig und unbeteiligt wie möglich sei. Andere versuchten, dem Assistenten eine aktive Rolle zuzuweisen, bis hin zur Einbindung in die musikalische Improvisation. Auf die unterschiedlichen Konsequenzen, die dies für den musiktherapeutischen Prozeß hat, werde ich später zurückkommen.

Häufig geschieht es auch, daß sich Probleme gerade daraus ergeben, daß der Assistent eine andere Vorstellung von seiner Rolle hat als der Therapeut. Die meisten Musiktherapeuten werden Situationen kennen, in denen ein wohlmeinender Assistent, in dem Versuch, zu „helfen", sämtliche Pausen des Therapeuten füllt, etwa dem Kind Trommelschlegel in die Hand drückt oder die alte Dame vehement auffordert, mitzusingen. Manchmal wird der Assistent außerhalb der Musiktherapie eine andere Rolle einnehmen müssen als innerhalb, was eine große Herausforderung sein kann. In vielen Fällen hilft sicherlich nur ganz direkte Kommunikation und eine Erklärung, was die Musiktherapie bezweckt und was sie nicht bezweckt und wie der Assistent diesen Prozeß unterstützen sollte.

Oft muß die Rolle des Assistenten immer wieder neu verhandelt und im Laufe des Prozesses neu geklärt werden. Ein Kollege berichtete mir von einer Situation, als er mit einem behinderten Jungen und einem Assistenten arbeitete. Musiktherapeut und Assistent waren übereingekommen, daß letzterer eine passive Rolle einnehmen würde, sich lediglich in die Ecke setzen und nicht ins Geschehen eingreifen würde. Doch je mehr der Assistent versuchte, sich zurückzuhalten, desto vehementer versuchte der Junge, seine Aufmerksamkeit zu bekommen, bis er schließlich fast ausschließlich auf den Assistenten fixiert war. Eine Änderung der Rollen – d.h. eine aktive Einbindung des Assistenten in das Geschehen – löste dieses Problem.

Nun kommen wir auf die oben gestellte Frage zurück, ob der Assistent ein Teil des therapeutischen Prozesses ist oder nicht. Ist er es, fällt unter „therapeutische Beziehung" dann auch die Beziehung zwischen Assistent und Klient? Und falls ja, wie sollte mit dieser

Erweiterung der therapeutischen Beziehung umgegangen werden? Sollten Gefühle zwischen Klienten und Assistenten, das Verhalten der beiden zueinander, Übertragung und Gegenübertragung thematisiert werden oder nicht?

Klar ist, daß allein die Anwesenheit des Assistenten einen Einfluß haben wird auf Verhalten und Emotionen des Klienten, sowie auf die Übertragungen und Gegenübertragungen, die sich im Raum abspielen. Unter Umständen ist der neutrale Boden, der der Therapieraum sein soll, mit einem Mal nicht mehr so neutral – zumal, wenn der Assistent im Leben des Klienten eine weitere Rolle spielt, oder wenn der Assistent und der Klient bereits mit einer „Vorgeschichte" in die Musiktherapie kommen.

In einer Sonderschule arbeitete ich mit einem Mädchen im Teenageralter, das mir aufgrund von aggressivem Verhalten in seiner Klasse überwiesen worden war. Wie bei Peter, von dem ich oben berichtete, kam eine Assistentin mit in die Musiktherapie, um meine Sicherheit zu schützen – denn das Mädchen hatte in der Vergangenheit eine Lehrerin so heftig attackiert, daß diese ärztliche Hilfe benötigte. Im Laufe der Zeit stellte sich dann heraus, daß die Haltung der Assistentin dem Mädchen gegenüber das aggressive Verhalten geradezu bewirkte und herausforderte – im Sinne einer sich selbst erfüllenden Prophezeiung. Ich befand mich also in einer Zwickmühle. Einerseits konnte ich, meiner eigenen Sicherheit wegen, mit dem Mädchen nicht alleine arbeiten. Andererseits schien die Erwartungshaltung der Assistentin genau das Verhalten in der Klientin hervorzurufen, aufgrund dessen sie zu mir geschickt worden war. Die Situation ließ sich erst lösen, als die Schule mich mit einem tragbaren Notrufknopf ausstattete, mit dem ich jederzeit Hilfe anfordern konnte, so daß die direkte Anwesenheit der Assistentin nicht mehr notwendig war.

Doch machen wir uns nichts vor – nicht nur der Klient wird durch die Anwesenheit des Assistenten in seinem Verhalten und in seinen Gefühlen beeinflußt werden. Auch der Therapeut wird in aller Regel anders handeln, anders reagieren und anders fühlen, sobald eine dritte Person sich im Raum befindet – gleichgültig, ob der Assistent eine aktive oder passive Rolle einnimmt. Möglicherweise fühlt sich der Therapeut stärker beobachtet, oder es entstehen Konkurrenz- oder Neidgefühle. Es kann sein, daß der Therapeut stärker als gewöhnlich den Druck verspürt, sich zu beweisen – was ebenfalls nicht ohne Einfluß auf das therapeutische Geschehen bleiben kann. Übertragung und Gegenübertragung können auch zwischen Assistent und Therapeut entstehen, werden aller Wahrscheinlichkeit nach aber nicht näher betrachtet oder ausgesprochen werden – ebenso, wie das auch der Fall sein kann, wenn es um Übertragung und Gegenübertragung zwischen Assistent und Klient geht.

Weiterhin ist es nicht ausgeschlossen, daß der Assistent die Haltung des Therapeuten gegenüber dem Klienten beeinflußt – und sei dies auf einer unbewußten Ebene. Es wird für die Wahrnehmung des Therapeuten einen Unterschied machen, ob der Assistent entspannt lächelnd mit dem Klienten zur Tür hereinkommt oder ob er gestreßt wirkt und dem Klienten ärgerliche Blicke zuwirft.

Doch die Anwesenheit des Assistenten hat nicht nur Konsequenzen für die therapeutische Beziehung, sondern in der Regel auch für die Rahmenbedingungen der Musiktherapie.

Da ist das Thema Schweigepflicht. Die Musiktherapiesitzung sollte ja eigentlich ein geschützter Raum sein, innerhalb dessen der Klient sich gefahrlos frei bewegen, neue Dinge ausprobieren kann etc. Doch durch die Anwesenheit einer weiteren Person verschiebt sich die Grenze – selbst dann, wenn klar ist, daß sich der Assistent seinerseits an die Schweigepflicht halten wird.

Die Anwesenheit eines Assistenten kann es schwieriger machen, die gewohnten Rahmenbedingungen zu schützen – etwa, wenn der Assistent es nicht gewohnt ist, daß Kollegen nicht stören dürfen oder daß er sein Handy ausgeschaltet halten muß, oder wenn der Assistent mit dem Hausmeister abgesprochen hat, daß dieser nebenbei die Heizung reparieren kann. In solchen Fällen hilft, wieder einmal, nur direkte Kommunikation.

Deutlich wird vor allem eines: ob man es möchte oder nicht, die Anwesenheit des Assistenten wird zwangsläufig einen Einfluß auf den therapeutischen Prozeß haben. Dies ist auch unabhängig davon, ob man auf eine aktive oder eine passive Rolle des Assistenten im Geschehen hinarbeitet. Wie viele Beispiele deutlich gemacht haben, wird es dem Assistenten selbst bei größter Zurückhaltung kaum möglich sein, im Raum anwesend zu sein, ohne die Dinge in irgend einer Weise zu beeinflussen, die geschehen.

Die Frage, die sich stellt, ist also nicht, ob der Assistent einen Einfluß auf den therapeutischen Prozeß hat, sondern welchen, und wie der Musiktherapeut damit umgehen kann.

Kommen wir zurück zu der Frage, welche Konsequenzen die Entscheidung haben kann, ob man dem Assistenten eine aktive oder eine passive Rolle zuweist.

Beide Möglichkeiten werfen ganz unterschiedliche Fragen und Probleme auf. Entscheidet der Therapeut sich dafür, dem Assistenten eine passive Rolle zuzuweisen, sozusagen möglichst so zu tun, als sei dieser überhaupt nicht da, dann kann es sein, daß ein Teil des Geschehens im Raum ausgeblendet wird – was durchaus einen negativen Einfluß auf den Prozeß haben kann, etwa auf die Gefühle, die entstehen, und auf Übertragung und Gegenübertragung. Es kann zu einer Situation kommen, in der „Tabuthemen" entstehen – Dinge, die im Raum eine Rolle spielen, die aber nicht an- oder ausgesprochen werden können, weil sie die Anwesenheit des Assistenten betreffen.

Entscheidet man sich dagegen dafür, dem Assistenten eine aktive Rolle zuzuweisen, dann kann dies wiederum ebenfalls eine ganze Palette an Fragen, Herausforderungen und potentiellen Schwierigkeiten aufwerfen.

Nicht immer besteht aus zeitlichen Gründen die Möglichkeit, sich mit dem Assistenten über seine Rolle auszutauschen oder ihn so ausreichend über Musiktherapie zu informieren, so daß ihm eine aktive Rolle übertragen werden kann. Nicht alle Assistenten fühlen sich mit einer aktiven Rolle wohl, leicht kann es zu einem Gefühl von Überforderung kommen. Manchen Assistenten wiederum fehlt das Gespür für den therapeutischen Prozeß, sie beginnen möglicherweise, unsensible Kommentare zu machen oder auf andere Art unwissentlich kontraproduktiv zu handeln.

Werden die Beziehungen aller Beteiligten untereinander als Teil des Prozesses betrachtet, dann stellt sich die Frage, wie mit Gefühlen zwischen Therapeut und Assistent umgegangen werden soll, die das Geschehen beeinflussen – zum Beispiel die musikalische Improvisation, falls der Assistent an dieser teilnimmt. Sollen sie ausgesprochen werden? Wann und auf welche Weise? Kann der Assistent damit umgehen? Besteht die Gefahr, daß der Fokus sich so sehr vom Klienten weg verschiebt, daß das eigentliche Ziel der Musiktherapie aus den Augen verloren wird?

Beide Möglichkeiten werfen also ganz unterschiedliche Herausforderungen und potentielle Schwierigkeiten auf.

Dennoch birgt die Anwesenheit des Assistenten auch Chancen in sich, die der Musiktherapeut sich für den therapeutischen Prozeß zunutze machen kann.

Es kann durchaus sein, daß das Nachdenken über die Rolle des Assistenten dazu führt, daß über den gesamten therapeutischen Prozeß, über die Beziehungen und Gefühle und Übertragungsmechanismen auf einer tieferen Ebene nachgedacht wird. Auf diese Weise können auch Erkenntnisse zutage kommen, die ohne die Anwesenheit des Assistenten nicht möglich gewesen wären.

In einer der Sonderschulen in England, in der ich arbeitete, leitete ich eine Gruppe mit vier autistischen Jugendlichen und einer Assistentin. Das Ziel, das ich mir für diese Jugendlichen gesetzt hatte, war es, ihr Bewußtsein für unterschiedliche Gefühle und deren Äußerung zu stärken. Der von mir eingeschlagene Weg bestand darin, mit der Gruppe Improvisationen in verschiedenen Stimmungen zu machen, Bilder mit unterschiedlichen Gesichtsausdrücken zuordnen zu lassen, die Schüler berichten zu lassen, wie sie sich gerade fühlten und Musik welcher Stimmung sie sich von der Gruppe wünschten, etc. Was mich eine lange Zeit über wunderte war, daß die Schüler immer wieder nach fröhlicher Musik fragten – selbst wenn sie sich ganz offensichtlich nicht in fröhlicher Stimmung befanden.

Eines Tages, als einer der Schüler gerade einen Wutanfall hatte, mit dem Fuß aufstampfte und mit geballter Faust auf eine Trommel schlug, wies die Assistentin ihn zurecht mit den Worten: „Jetzt benimm dich aber, und sei fröhlich!"

Nach meiner anfänglich leicht schockierten Reaktion auf solch eine pädagogische Maßnahme begann sich mir das tiefere Problem zu erschließen, das diese Gruppe hatte. In weiteren Gesprächen mit der Assistentin wurde deutlich, daß die Strategie, die in der Klasse mit diesen Jugendlichen verfolgt wurde, folgende war: immer wieder wurden die Schüler für das Ausdrücken von wütenden oder traurigen Gefühlen getadelt und dazu angehalten, nur fröhliche Gefühle zum Ausdruck zu bringen.

Hätte ich diese Gruppe nicht zusammen mit der Assistentin geleitet, die dann eines Tages mit einer zunächst völlig unpassend erscheinenden Bemerkung herausplatzte, so wäre ich niemals auf diese Erklärung für das Verhalten der vier Jugendlichen gestoßen.

Anhand dieser und ähnlicher Situationen wurde mir mit der Zeit folgendes deutlich: vieles, das oberflächlich als eine, durch die Anwesenheit des Assistenten bedingte, Störung der Musiktherapie betrachtet werden kann, birgt unter Umständen auch eine Chance in sich. Indem man sich mit diesen Reibungen und ihren Ursachen auseinandersetzt, kann der Blick weiter geöffnet werden, als dies ohne die Anwesenheit des Assistenten möglich gewesen wäre. Der

Assistent kann eine Brücke darstellen zwischen dem Klienten und seinem Leben außerhalb der Musiktherapiesitzung.

Selbstverständlich ist es nicht in allen Fällen möglich, mit Schwierigkeiten dieser Art produktiv umzugehen. Natürlich wird es auch Situationen geben, in denen ein Assistent schlicht und einfach den Prozeß behindert, ohne daß dieses Problem gelöst werden kann. Nicht immer ist eine Zusammenarbeit zwischen einem bestimmten Musiktherapeuten und einem bestimmten Assistenten möglich.

In der Regel jedoch kann der musiktherapeutische Prozess an Tiefe, an Ehrlichkeit und an Unmittelbarkeit gewinnen, wenn wir beginnen, die Situation als das anzunehmen und zu betrachten, was sie ist, wenn wir bewußt unsere Entscheidungen anders treffen, als wir sie ohne die Anwesenheit des Assistenten getroffen hätten, und wenn wir den Einfluß des Assistenten auf den Prozeß in unsere Überlegungen mit einbeziehen.

Dann werden wir auch nicht in die Falle tappen, uns vorzugaukeln, die Situation sei etwas, das sie nicht sein kann: eine traditionelle therapeutische Zweierbeziehung.

References

- Bruscia, K. E. (1988) (ed.) *The Dynamics of Music Psychotherapy*, Gilsum, NH: Barcelona

- Bunt, L. and Hoskyns, S. (2002) (ed.) *The Handbook of Music Therapy,* Hove: Brunner- Routledge

- Corey, G., Corey, M. S. and Callanan, P. (1988) *Issues and Ethics in the Helping Professions*, Pacific Grove, CA: Brooks / Cole

- Eschen, J.T. (2002) *Analytical Music Therapy,* London: Routledge

- Gray, A. (1994) *An Introduction to the Therapeutic Frame*, London: Routledge

- Klauber, T. (1999): *The significance of trauma and other factors.* In: Alvarez, A. and Reid, S. (ed): *Autism and Personality,* Findings from the Tavistock Autism Workshop. London: Routledge

- Mc Guire, D. and Mc Guire, D. (2000) *Linking Parents to Play Therapy*, Philadelphia: Brunner- Routledge

- Priestley, M. (1994) *Essays on Analytical Music Therapy,* Phoenixville: Barcelona

- Schumacher, K. (1994) *Musiktherapie mit autistischen Kindern*, Stuttgart: G. Fischer

Appendix I: Questionnaire for music therapists about their experiences with assistants in their sessions

1. Do you, during your music therapy work, ever work with another person in the room, who is neither a co-therapist nor parent nor another client? (e.g. support assistant, medical supervisor, translator, etc)
(Never / Seldom / Sometimes / Often / Usually)

If the answer is never, go straight to question 6!

2. Which of these roles have third people had in your sessions?
(Never / Seldom / Sometimes / Often / Usually) Please specify for each.

- Assistant with practical things (such as holding a drum)

- Assistant with behaviour management

- Assistant with medical issues

- Translator

- Student or person who wants to find out about music therapy

- Another professional who wants to observe the client in the music therapy context

- Any others?

3. Do you feel that the presence of the third person has any impact on the therapeutic process?
(Never / Seldom / Sometimes / Often / Usually)

If yes, which of the following do you feel is being influenced? (Never / Seldom / Sometimes / Often / Usually)Please specify for each

- The actual music therapy approach

- The therapeutic relationship itself

- Therapist's perception of the client

- Transference and countertransference

- The relationship between the therapist and the work setting (school, care home, hospital)

- The boundaries of the music therapy work

- The willingness to take risks or be open to the yet unknown

- Any others that you can think of? Please specify.

4. If you work with a person who is present for practical support (such as medical staff, or translator), would you tend to regard the third person as

- an integral part of the therapeutic process, or
- an observer to the therapeutic process?

Would you, as a tendency, work towards giving the person an active role in the session (apart from the practical task they are there to do), or would you work towards making their role as passive and held back as possible?

Would you tend to

- allow them to take a musical role, i.e. play an instrument or sing?
(Never / Seldom / Sometimes / Often / Usually)

- allow them to contribute verbally?
(Never / Seldom / Sometimes / Often / Usually)

- encourage them to contribute verbally?
(Never / Seldom / Sometimes / Often / Usually)

- work through issues that have arisen out of the presence of the third person
    - During the session
    - After the session?

- musically acknowledge their presence? (e.g. include them in hello or goodbye songs, or otherwise take their presence into account musically?)

- verbally acknowledge their presence?

Would this differ between group sessions and individual sessions?

5. How would you describe your approach to music therapy? E.g. person-centred, psychoanalytically informed, behavioural.

6. Which setting (s) do you work in, and with which client and age groups?

7. Do you have any other thoughts or comments on this subject that might be interesting?

8. I am very interested in hearing about people's experiences on this subject, more directly. If you would be willing to arrange for a conversation, or if you have any more interesting thoughts or things to share, please drop me an email or give me a ring.

I am very grateful that you have taken the time to answer these questions.

Appendix II: Assistants in music therapy sessions

Dear assistant,

I'm currently doing a project to see how work relationships between music therapists and music therapy assistants could be improved, what is helpful to the work, and what isn't. I, as well as a lot of my colleagues, do a lot of work with the help of assistants in their sessions, yet this has found no recognition in music therapy literature so far.

I would be very interested in your comments, thoughts and ideas. If you were able to spare a few minutes and answer the following questions, then I would highly appreciate this!

You don't need to write your name onto the questionnaire, just put it back into my pigeon hole anonymously!

- What has been your best and what has been your worst experience in a music therapy session?

- What have you found difficult about your role as an assistant in a music therapy session? What could the music therapist have done to help this? What have you enjoyed about being an assistant in a music therapy session?

- Often, music therapy and classroom teaching differ a lot in approach, boundaries, in what pupils are and are not allowed to do, etc. etc. Did you find these differences difficult? If so, which particular difficulties do you feel arose out of this situation? What could the music therapist have done to make any clashes as workable as possible?

- What do you feel the music therapist could do to make your task easier or more enjoyable?

Appendix III: Information leaflet on music therapy for assistants

For assistants who join music therapy sessions
(Britta Schmidt, March 2003)

Recently, I have been asked by several assistants whether I could tell them a bit more about what the music therapy sessions are about, what they should be doing in there, etc. I then started feeling that it might be useful to just write down a few things and pass them on to anybody who might come into a music therapy session.

Do feel free to ask me more. I am open for communication, as I hope people know.

What is music therapy for?

Music therapy aims at helping children who have particularly strong needs or difficulties. Music therapy can help with a child's communication skills, confidence, creativity and self expression, motor skills or language development. Generally, through the use of improvised music, any of these aims can be worked towards. The children will get the chance to play easy instruments and the therapist will improvise along. Music therapy is based on the fact that the ability to respond to music is usually unaffected by disability, therefore music can often reach a child who finds communication difficult.

What exactly happens within a session will vary and depend on the particular child or group and their needs - some sessions will be more structured than others, some music therapy work will be more directive than others.

What is the difference between music therapy and music lessons?

Music teaching aims at improving musical skills. Music therapy does not do that. Music therapy has non-musical aims. It does not aim at teaching children songs, or at making them play particular instruments in particular ways. Through the use of mainly improvised music, the session will flexibly adapt to the child's needs and to the situation and work towards non-musical aims.

How could an assistant support a music therapy session?

It is often not necessary to do an awful lot at all. Sometimes it could just be enough to be there, relax and enjoy what's happening, and step in only when necessary.

There is no pressure to be 'doing' things all the time. Sometimes doing less (and letting the child make the choices, taking the lead or finding out what their preferences or needs are) can actually be more helpful! Disabled people might have a different inner speed or rhythm. It might be helpful to give them the time THEY need. This might mean that we have to change the speed that we normally operate in. Sometimes music therapy sessions are about creating a little bit of space for them in which they can make their own decisions and find their own ways of expressing themselves, in their own pace.

Often it is helpful if an assistant simply supports children with whatever they have chosen to do. This could include picking up an instrument that a child has accidentally dropped and cannot reach, or holding the guitar if a child chooses to strum it (rather than taking their hand and making them strum it).

The level of direction within the session might vary a lot. Sometimes the children might be asked to actually stay in their chairs - sometimes they might be free to use the room as they choose to. Sometimes it will be appropriate to encourage a child to play an instrument, even if they do not take any initiative to do so; sometimes it will be appropriate to give them full freedom in their choices (which may well include not playing anything at all).

Generally, it is helpful to me if the assistant simply supports whatever the boundaries of the session happen to be.

If in doubt – just ask.

Assistants are welcome to join in with the music - play instruments, or join in with the singing if they wish. But again, there is no pressure to do so.

Britta Schmidt-Robyn has worked as a music therapist since 2001. She has experience in many different areas, including special needs schools, mental health, neurology and dementia care. This book is based on her MA dissertation, which she completed for Anglia Polytechnic University in Cambridge, England. She currently lives and works in Berlin, Germany.